COMMUNICATION STRATEGIES 3

Jun Liu

Tracy Davis

Susanne Rizzo

Australia • Brazil • Japan • Korea • Mexico • Singapore • Spain • United Kingdom • United States

Communication Strategies 3
Jun Liu, Tracy Davis, and Susanne Rizzo

Publishing Director: Paul Tan
Editorial Manager: Andrew Robinson
Editor: Andrew Jessop

Senior Product Manager: Michael Cahill
Interior Design: Pixel Production Works
Printer: Seng Lee Press

The publisher would like to thank The Kobal Collection for their permission to reproduce photographs on the following pages:

6: The Devil Wears Prada 20th Century Fox / The Kobal Collection and Barry Wetcher; 12: Final Fantasy: The Spirits Within Chris Lee Prod/Square Co / The Kobal Collection; 18: Thank You for Smoking Fox Searchlight / The Kobal Collection; 24: Endurance The Kobal Collection; 30: Cellular New Line/Electric Entertainment / The Kobal Collection / Richard Foreman; 42: Pay it Forward Bel Air/WB / The Kobal Collection / David James; 48: Who Killed the Electric Car? Electric Entertainment/Sony / The Kobal Collection; 54: Murderball MTV Films / The Kobal Collection; 60: Good Will Hunting Matt Damon Miramax / The Kobal Collection; 66: School of Rock Paramount / The Kobal Collection / Andrew Schwartz; 72: Bend It Like Beckham Bend It Films/Film Council / The Kobal Collection / Christine Parry; 78: Must Love Dogs Warner Bros. / The Kobal Collection / Claudette Barius; 84: Freaky Friday Walt Disney Pictures / The Kobal Collection / Ron Batzdorf; 90: Dante's Peak Universal / The Kobal Collection / Ben Glass

The publisher would like to thank the following for their permission to reproduce photographs on the following pages:

© 2007 Jupiterimages Corporation: 07, 09, 11, 15, 19, 21, 23, 25, 27, 28, 29, 31, 33, 34, 35, 37, 39, 41, 49, 51, 53, 61, 63, 65, 67, 70, 73, 75, 76, 79, 81, 83, 85, 87, 88, 89, 91, 93, 94.

© 2007 Getty Images Sales Singapore Pte Ltd: 10, 13, 16, 19, 23(top), 43, 45, 46, 47, 69.

Please note, that all people shown are models and are used only for illustrative purposes.

For permission to use material from this text or product, email to **asia.publishing@cengage.com**

ISBN-13: 978-981-265-914-9
ISBN-10: 981-265-914-5

Cengage Learning Asia Pte Ltd
5 Shenton Way #01-01
UIC Building
Singapore 068808
Tel: (65) 6410 1200
Fax: (65) 6410 1208

Cengage Learning products are represented in Canada by Nelson Education, Ltd.

For product information, visit **cengageasia.com**

Printed in Singapore
1 2 3 4 5 6 7 8 9 10 11 – 11 10 09 08 07

FOREWORD

Learners are often able to strike up a conversation in English, but after a few minutes, they soon get tongue-tied when the conversation moves beyond the surface level. I firmly believe that to overcome this, students should concentrate on reaching a reasonably high level of communicative competence as quickly as possible. Once this is attained, learners will have elevated themselves from language learners to language users and will then be in a better position to build on this knowledge. They will also be better prepared to deal with the range of exams that many of them now face, including CET 4, IELTS, or TOEFL.

Only by getting into the substance of communication can we move beyond formulaic English and become language users. This textbook series is designed to enable you to be excellent strategic language users. It is my hope that you will enjoy using the book to further your communication strategies and become excellent users of English in real communication.

Jun Liu
Professor and Head of English Department
University of Arizona

ACKNOWLEDGMENTS

I would like to thank my co-authors of this book, Tracy Davis and Suzanne Rizzo, for their great collaboration and enthusiastic work while teaching English at Shantou University. I am indebted to everyone at Cengage Learning, in particular, Paul Tan, Andrew Robinson, Andrew Jessop, and Hoi Kin Chiu, for their trust, encouragement, and great assistance in the process of the book production.

I would also like to thank the professionals who have offered invaluable comments and suggestions during the development of the course, in particular:

Chen Lijiang – *Associate Professor, Shanghai International Studies University*
Fan Xiangtao – *Associate Professor, Nanjing University of Aeronautics and Astronautics*
Gao Dexin – *Associate Professor , Shandong Liyi Normal University*
Jia Zhongheng – *Associate Professor, Tong Ji University*
Li Zhiling – *Professor, Shandong Agricultural University*
Quan Jianqiang – *Vice-Dean of English Department, East China Normal University*
Tao Qing – *Professor, Shanghai Jiao Tong University*
Wan Hua – *Dean of English Department, Shanghai University*
Wei Xiangqing – *Professor, Nanjing University*
Zhang Yi – *Dean of English Department, East China Normal University*
Zong Ruikun – *Professor, Shanghai Xing Jian College*

Jun Liu

TABLE OF CONTENTS

DISCUSSION STRATEGIES		SPEECHES
Expressing negative comments diplomatically	It's not my favorite. It's not the most flattering. You may want to reconsider…	New dress code
Paraphrasing	What you're saying is...? Let me get this straight, you mean…? Okay, so you think that...?	Debate
Making direct and indirect requests	Could you…? Wouldn't it be nice if…? Someone really should…	Take a stand
Complaining	You shouldn't… It isn't fair. I'm sick and tired of…	Interview a famous athlete
Showing that you are listening	Uh huh Sounds good You're kidding	Here's what I'd say
Making requests	Would you mind ____ing...? Could you possibly...? Would you (please)...?	A lesson
Offering to help	Can I help you? Would you like any help ____ing? Let me give you a hand.	Ask for support
Interrupting	Can I (just) say… Right and you know that… I'm sorry, but…	Staying healthy
Asking not to be interrupted	Could I please finish? Hold on (a second), let me finish. Wait, I'm almost done.	My own extreme sport
Conceding but disagreeing	You have a point, but… You may be right, but… That may be true, but…	Presentations
Strongly disagreeing	That just isn't so. I think you have it wrong. I see it differently.	You are the teacher
Support your opinions	What about the… I know for a fact… You can't deny that…	Interview on unfair treatment
Saying no nicely	Sorry, I have other plans. Thanks for asking, but… Thanks, but I'm not (really) fond of...	Talk show
Giving advice	Maybe you should consider ____ing... You could (always).... I'm told that ... is good.	Story telling
Giving bad news	I regret to inform you that... Unfortunately... I'm (really) sorry, but...	Weather report

Dress Code

Does what you wear really matter that much? We asked a group of young people, and here is an extract from their conversation:

TARA: I think it matters a lot. People judge us based on first appearance and how we dress is a big part of creating a good first impression. When I see someone walking down the street, I notice what they are wearing. How people dress says a lot about them.

KEN: That's partly because it's drilled into us from such an early age! When I was in high school, the teachers used to tell us our uniform was a symbol of the school's values and that it created a sense of unity and collective pride. I didn't really care about that, but on the flip side, I do think having a uniform helped me as I didn't have to worry about what to wear when I was getting ready, half asleep in the morning.

EVA: When I was at school, I didn't have to wear a uniform, but my school was still super strict about what we wore. They used the same 'collective pride' argument and said the dress code helped students focus on their classes rather than how they look. They also said it would help prepare us for the future because whether we like it or not, dress codes are everywhere.

TARA: I agree with that last point. I mean there are dress codes for most situations even if they aren't written, right? My appearance at work is important. If I don't keep to my company's dress code, I could lose my job.

TOMAS: That's crazy. I don't think there should be dress codes. It tells us that society values conformity, it says, 'Be like everyone else.' I like to express myself through my clothes and show some kind of individuality. How I dress is part of my identity. A dress code stifles our freedom and our ability to develop a sense of self.

KEN: Yes, but it does matter what we wear. It's about knowing what the expectations are, whether you're in an office or at a wedding or a funeral. We think about what to wear and how we look when we're out with friends, right? It's about knowing what's appropriate in a given situation — casual, formal, whatever. I mean, would you trust a doctor dressed in scruffy clothes and showing a lot of tattoos?

TOMAS: But who determines what's appropriate? I have a small tattoo on my arm. At a job interview last week, someone told me I'd have to cover it up if I wanted a job in sales. My tattoo has nothing to do with my ability to sell cars.

EVA: Yes, but you didn't get the job, did you, which may just prove the point. Our appearance, especially how we dress, is taken as a sign of respect; respect for ourselves, for our school, or employer. Like it or not, people judge us by how we dress and take care of our appearance.

KEN: I have to say, if I was interviewing two people for the same job and one of them came to the interview in jeans and a T-shirt and the other came in a suit, I know who I'd be more likely to hire.

VOCABULARY

Here are some words that will be useful in this unit. How many do you know? Work with a partner to figure out the meaning of any words that you don't know.

appearance	dress code	judge
appropriate	expectations	respect for
casual	freedom	scruffy
collective	identity	stifle
comply with	inappropriate	symbol
conformity	individuality	uniform

What other words and phrases do you know related to the topic?

VOCABULARY ACTIVITIES

A. Fill in the blanks with words from the list above. Remember to use the correct word form.

1. Some people feel __stifled__ by strict dress codes. They want more __freedom__ to wear whatever they choose.
2. Other people feel uniforms are __a symbol__ of unity.
3. Like it or not, other people often judge you by your __appearance__
4. It's __inappropriate__ to wear jeans and a T-shirt to most job interviews.
5. Dress codes are everywhere. There are __expectations__ about what is acceptable in a situation such as at an office or at a party, for example.

B. Work with a partner. Make a list of adjectives you use to answer the following questions.

1. Think about different activities you do. What are the expectations for how you dress in those situations?
2. What do you or people you know wear to express their individuality?

Quick Fact

Mexico — In elementary and middle school, students have to wear uniforms, but not in high school.

GRAPHIC ORGANIZER

Think about different situations and what is appropriate to wear in each of them. Fill in your ideas. Then work with a partner and compare your ideas.

AT WORK

AT SCHOOL

A FAMILY DINNER AT HOME

DRESS CODE

A FIRST DATE

OTHER

POINTS OF VIEW *People DO judge a book by its cover.*

PRE-LISTENING QUESTIONS

1. From the title, "People DO judge a book by its cover" what do you think the characters will talk about?
2. What do the clothes we wear say about us?

SITUATION: *Amy had a bad experience at a shop recently.*

Amy I needed to buy a gift last weekend so I went shopping at that fancy new boutique. But no one would help me. I'm sure it's because of the way I was dressed; I had just come from my yoga class and I was still in my gym clothes.

Kim They probably thought you couldn't afford anything in the store. Didn't you feel out of place?

Amy Not at first, but I did start to feel really uncomfortable when they ignored me. Still, I can't believe that they would judge me from what I was wearing. I think that kind of discrimination based on first impressions is so silly.

Kim I know, but people size you up pretty quickly from what you wear. Once, my father invited me to a party at his company. He said it was casual so I wore shorts and a T-shirt. When I got there, everyone was wearing smart shirts and pants or skirts. My idea of casual and theirs were quite different. I got a lot of stares and my father was embarrassed. I just wanted to leave. It made me really self-conscious.

Amy I guess you're right, but…

Kim Speaking of first impressions, you're not going to wear your red dress tonight, are you?

Amy I was planning to. Why?

Kim Well, you may want to reconsider.

Amy Why? I really like that dress; it's my favorite.

Kim Yeah, well, it's okay for a nightclub, but maybe it's just a little too short and too tight for tonight's party. There'll be a lot of important people there.

Amy I like it and I feel good in it. I'm wearing it.

Kim Have it your way, but I'm sure everyone else will be dressed more conservatively.

CHECK FOR UNDERSTANDING

1. Why was Amy so upset?
2. What happened when she went to the party with her father?
3. Why does Kim think Amy's dress is unsuitable?

Work with a partner. Compare your answers.

Quick Fact
Japan — The number of students, who like school uniforms is on the rise as uniforms have become more fashionable.

PRACTICE AND DISCUSSION

PERSONALIZATION

Complete these sentences with your own ideas.

I can't stand it when…

I felt out of place when…

I just can't believe that…

People size you up pretty quickly from…

Now share your sentences with a classmate.

DISCUSSION STRATEGIES -
Expressing negative comments diplomatically

Listed below are ways to express negative feelings about what someone is wearing without hurting the other person's feelings. Can you think of other ways that you may have heard?

It's not my favorite.

It's unique.

What an interesting outfit.

You may want to reconsider…

I don't think anyone else has the same one/one like it.

It's not the most flattering.

It's different.

You will definitely stand out.

Quick Fact
China — Uniforms are usually supplied by the school if required.

Discussion Strategy in Action

Listen to the conversations. Does the person like what he/she is shown? What discussion strategy phrase does the speaker use?

	Conversation	The speaker		The speaker says:
1.	Tim	likes/doesn't like	his new shirt	_____
	Anne	likes/doesn't like	Tim's blue shirt	_____
2.	Jack	likes/doesn't like	Tom's new suit	_____
3.	Rita	likes/doesn't like	Carol's dress	_____
4.	Tim	likes/doesn't like	his _____	_____
	Jack	likes/doesn't like	_____	_____

Discussion Practice

Some of the people where you work are dressed inappropriately for the following situations. Convince them to conform to the company's dress code using the discussion strategies above.

1. They are meeting important customers today.
2. There is a staff party today. Staff can wear what they want as long as it still looks professional. Visitors from another company will be there.
3. They are wearing clothes similar to the company uniform, but in different colors.

ROLE PLAY

Work with a partner. Look at the situations below. Decide your roles.
Create dialogs using the discussion strategies.

1. You and your partner are going to a formal party and you think his/her outfit is all wrong.

2. You and your best friend are shopping for clothes for a new job. Your friend shows you an outfit. You think it's all wrong for an office job.

3. You receive an expensive, red leather jacket that you don't like from your friend.

> **Brainstorming:**
>
> In what situations would you discuss someone's clothing or appearance?
>
> Is it ever better not to say anything?

ACTIVITY

Look at the following pictures. Decide what occasion the people are dressed for and why. Discuss your choices with your classmates. Do you agree?

SPEECHES - New dress code

You work for a high tech company. The company has been discussing changing the dress code. Some people feel a more casual dress code will help people feel more creative and think it will boost the company's image. Other people disagree and are concerned about looking too casual, especially the sales representatives.

Work with a partner. Come up with a dress code for the company.
Then present it to your classmates. Questions to consider:

• What are examples of appropriate and inappropriate "casual" dress?

• Should all employees have the same dress code?

• Should the dress code be the same every day?

• Should there be any penalties for not complying with a dress code?

• Should the dress code include things such as hair style, tattoos etc?

> **Quick Fact**
> Kenya — Uniforms are required in government schools.

CONSOLIDATION AND RECYCLING

BUILDING VOCABULARY

Look at the list of words below. Work with a partner. Complete the chart with the appropriate forms of each word. Check, using your dictionary. Some words may not have all forms.

appearance   symbol   unity

regulation   conformity   stifle

Do the same for other new vocabulary words found in this unit.

NOUN	VERB	ADJECTIVE
individual, individuality, individualism	*individualize*	*individual*

Write sentences using each word form in the chart.
Work with a partner to compare your sentences.

WRITING

"You are what you wear"

"Dress for success"

"Clothes make a person"

Consider the above expressions then write to explain whether you think that what you wear is important, whether you think other people judge you by what you wear, and whether it matters to you.

Support your ideas. Then work with a partner. Exchange texts and comment on each other's ideas.

REFLECTION

1. What purpose do dress codes play in society?
2. You have probably seen someone dressed inappropriately for a situation.
   How did you feel and what did you do?
3. Describe an experience where you have felt uncomfortable/self-conscious because of the way you were dressed.

Video Games

Video games are big business and people from all walks of life play them. While most people can see the attraction of video games and would agree that educational games are actually very useful, video games in general, still have a pretty bad reputation.

There are those who see video games only as violent, addictive, and a complete waste of time. These people also point to gaming as being a cause of students' low grades and responsible for bad habits such as swearing and violent behavior.

For every opponent of video games though, there seem to be plenty of supporters who can't wait for the latest innovation and their next chance to play; whether it's playing together with friends, playing online, either as part of an online team or alone, or just taking a moment to play at home to help them switch off and relax a bit.

More and more people now seek out places such as restaurants with video games at the tables so that they can continue gaming in common social situations. Opponents say these people are obsessed and use this to show that gaming has a negative impact on some people's ability to socialize in real life situations.

Dance Dance Revolution, or DDR as it is more commonly referred to, is one video game that has managed to avoid a lot of the negative stereotypes associated with video games. There are no weapons, no blood or gore, in fact, no violence of any kind. And while people may get hooked on playing DDR type games, it is almost impossible to play for too long because it is so physically demanding.

The concept is simple: as arrows scroll up or across the screen, the player must step on certain corresponding positions on the special game pad on the floor. Players need to step to the beat of the music to score the most points. The result is a workout while gaming.

Players of DDR are anything but lazy – at least good players. That's probably the biggest difference from the usual stereotype of a gamer; someone, usually male, sitting slouched in a chair, eyes fixed on the screen, with only his fingers moving as he concentrates on the game.

Different forms of DDR have been added to many school physical fitness programs worldwide. They are also found in arcades and available for use with home computers and various video game systems; DDR has become quite a craze.

However, it does have its detractors. One of the biggest drawbacks is the song lyrics. In some versions of the game the music may contain profanity and some people feel this makes them inappropriate for younger players, a common complaint leveled against many other video games, too. People are also concerned that by encouraging children to use DDR machines in video arcades, children are exposed to other, less wholesome video games.

VOCABULARY

Here are some words that will be useful in this unit. How many do you know? Work with a partner to figure out the meaning of any words that you don't know.

addictive	gamers	innovation	scroll
arcade	gaming	lyrics	slouched
controller	gore	obsessed	versions
drawback	hooked on	opponent	violent
game pad	inappropriate	profanity	wholesome

What other words and phrases do you know related to the topic?

VOCABULARY ACTIVITIES

A. Fill in the blanks with words from the list above. Remember to use the correct word form.

1. The students went to the video _____ after school everyday to play video games.
2. Some song lyrics are profound so DDR is _____ for young players.
3. Companies usually come out with new _____ of games that are even more successful.
4. The nice thing about a _____ is that you use your feet to play.
5. Video games aren't really_____ . They're fun to play, but most people can control themselves.
6. One _____ of some video games is they are violent.

B. One way to learn more vocabulary is to group words together. Some of the words above are about equipment, some describe video games, and some describe players.

Work with a partner. Choose a category and ask your partner to say a word from that category. Take turns.

Example: Student A: equipment   *Student B: player*
Student B: game pad   *Student A: a gamer*

GRAPHIC ORGANIZER

Create a mind map that shows your ideas about video games. Then work with a partner and compare your ideas.

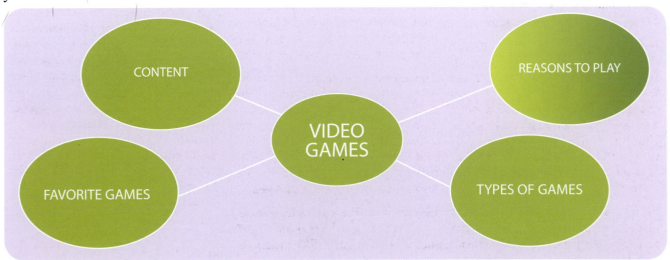

PRE-LISTENING QUESTIONS

1. What do you do in your spare time?
2. Have you ever thought that you "wasted" your time doing something fun? When? What did you do? What should you have been doing instead?

SITUATION: *Trey is considering deleting all the games from his computer.*

Trey	I think I'm going to delete all the video games from my computer. I spend too much time playing and at the end of the day, I have nothing to show for it.
Scot	So, let me get this straight, you're going to do that because you think they're a waste of time?
Trey	Yeah, basically.
Scot	For me, video games are a great way to relax. I just step out of my life and into the game. I need some time to play every day, to forget about all the stress in my life.
Trey	It's up to you how you want to spend your time. I know if play them too much, I actually feel more stressed, especially if I don't get other, more important things done.
Scot	You might be right. But you're stressed if you play and stressed if you don't, so you might as well play. I think video games are a great way to kick back and relax. I like to play as soon as I get home and on the weekends. There are a lot worse things to do. Besides, at the end of the day, I know I am good at something, even if it's just being a gamer. It makes me feel better about myself.
Trey	So what you're saying is you play video games to build your self-confidence, right? All the violence, all the sneaking around and killing and you feel good about yourself afterwards?
Scot	Yes, I mean no, that's not exactly what I mean. I'm saying that knowing I'm good at something makes me happy. Anyway, not all video games are violent. They can be educational or develop skills like hand-eye coordination. Did you know that some studies have found that surgeons who regularly play computer games are better at operating modern surgery tools than those who don't play video games?
Trey	Interesting, maybe I'll check if my surgeon is a gamer if I ever have to have an operation. Anyway, it's up to you what you do. I just know I have to take a break and play less for a while.
Scot	Okay, but before you do that, there's a really cool game I want to show you.

Quick Fact
Around 56% of online gamers are male

CHECK FOR UNDERSTANDING

1. Why is Trey deleting his games?
2. What is the main reason Scot likes to play?
3. Why does Scot mention surgeons?
4. Do you think Trey will give up playing games altogether?
5. Who do you agree with more, Trey or Scott? Why?

Work with a partner. Compare your answers.

PRACTICE AND DISCUSSION

PERSONALIZATION

Complete these sentences with your own ideas.

> *I spend too much time...*
>
> *...is a great way to relax.*
>
> *...can cause stress.*
>
> *...is what makes me feel better.*
>
> *I just know I have to...*

Now share your sentences with a classmate.

DISCUSSION STRATEGIES - Paraphrasing

When someone is explaining something, the listener may restate (paraphrase) what the speaker said to make sure that he or she completely understands. The paraphrase is a simplified version of what the speaker said. The other speaker either confirms it *("Yes, that's what I mean")* or clarifies the point *("No, I mean...")*

Some phrases commonly used to start a paraphrase are:

What you're saying is...?　　　　　　**Let me get this straight, you mean...?**

Okay, so you think that...?　　　　　　**So, what you mean is...?**

In the end, you're saying...?　　　　　　**Are you telling me...?**

Can you add others that you may have heard?

Find the paraphrases used in the Points of View dialog.

Quick Fact
The average gamer plays 6.8 hours a week.

Discussion Strategy in Action

Listen to the conversations. One person paraphrases what he hears. Does he paraphrase it correctly? What phrase does the speaker start with?

Conversation	Paraphrased correctly	Phrase used
1.	yes / no	_____
2.	yes / no	_____
3.	yes / no	_____

Discussion Practice

Work with a partner. Look at the situations below. Decide your roles. Create dialogs using the discussion strategies. Take turns.

Student A: Choose one of the topics below. Give your opinion. Include several reasons.
Student B: Paraphrase Student A's opinion using one of the discussion strategies.

1. Violent video games should be banned.
2. Providing computer games for employees during their lunch break would help them relax.
3. Schools should control the amount of time students spend playing video games.

FURTHER ACTIVITIES

ROLE PLAY

Brainstorming:

What are good themes or ideas for video games?

What features are important in a video game?

What would be a good idea for an educational video game?

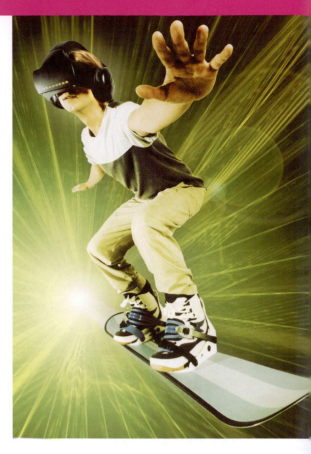

Student A: You have an idea for a new video game. Present it to a manufacturer.

Student B: Paraphrase the idea and ask questions to find out more details about the game.

Example:
Student A: My idea is a game about …
Student B: Let me get this straight. You want to make a video game that has …. in it?

ACTIVITY

Some countries provide ratings for video games. The rating tells people what age the video game is appropriate for and sometimes what kind of video game it is.

What are the most important things to consider when rating a video game?

1. _____   4. _____
2. _____   5. _____
3. _____   6. _____

What ages make good cut-off points for ratings?
Work in a small group. Create your own ratings system for video games.
Compare your ratings system with those created by other groups in your class.

Quick Fact
Around 35% of online gamers are under the age of 18.

SPEECHES - Debate

Because many young students are growing up surrounded by technology. They are used to getting information from the TV, computers, DVDs, and so on. Because of this, some people feel increasing the use of video games in school will help students learn more effectively. Others feel video games are creating poor learners and that playing video games should be discouraged. Some people also feel that many of the educational videos, especially those for very young children, are a waste of money.

Work with a partner. Come up with as many reasons as possible for and against increasing the use of video games in school. Take notes on your ideas.

Then hold a debate with another pair. Remember to argue both sides.

CONSOLIDATION AND RECYCLING

BUILDING VOCABULARY

Fill in the blanks.

Video games are played worldwide. People play at home, at Internet cafes or in video _____ . Some people feel that video games are dangerous and _____ . They worry kids will become _____ to playing video games all the time. Other people think video games can actually be used to improve academic results. Rather than thinking of video games as a waste of time, they see them as an opportunity for students to learn to think creatively, to problem-solve and to make connections between ideas. Some parents are concerned that playing video games will make their kids violent and socially isolated. They worry about their child sitting _____ over a desk, holding the game _____ all alone in the bedroom for hours at a time. But creators of video games say that many of the games, especially those played over the Internet, are designed for teams. The games require people to communicate. And, new _____ of games are coming out that bring people together even more. One _____ to some video games, though, is that the _____ to some songs are _____ for younger players. But creators of other video games say their games are educational across _____ . They say their games help people think. You just need to know which games to buy.

Work with a partner. Do you think video games can benefit all students?

WRITING

Imagine that you write an advice column called "Ask Me" in the local newspaper. Readers write letters asking for advice on different problems.

> Dear Ask Me,
> My 14-year-old daughter loves to play video games. She plays them in nearly all her spare time. Her grades are fine and she still hangs out with her friends, but between school, her friends, and the video games, I don't have any time with her myself. She loves her games and I don't want to make her stop playing them. But how can I spend more time with her?
>
> Yours sincerely,
> What should I do?

Write a response to the letter. Exchange your reply with a classmate. Compare your ideas.

REFLECTION

1. How has your opinion of video games changed during this unit?
2. What did you learn about a classmate that you did not know before?
3. Do you have a favorite video game?

UNIT 3

Advertising

Advertising is everywhere and many consumers around the world now feel overwhelmed. On its most basic level, advertising informs potential customers about a product and why they should buy it. This approach might continue to work for some basic, everyday products, but a simple message is not always enough so advertising has become much more sophisticated. Creativity and innovation are essential.

We often choose a product because the ad appeals to how we would like to see ourselves or the kind of lifestyle that is attractive to us: cool, sophisticated, relaxed, funny, or macho. Some of the most innovative advertising campaigns have been used by cigarette and drinks companies. They understood early on that it was more important to create a strong image that people would aspire to than to concentrate on directly promoting their products' qualities. They also realized that they could use advertising to counteract any negative publicity surrounding their products.

Advertisers have adopted more subtle techniques such as 'placing' their products in television programs, movies and books, paying money to have their product used or seen instead of their rivals'. They also contract glamorous or high profile celebrities to actively endorse the products as a spokesperson or at least be seen using the products. For example, sportswear and equipment companies sponsor top athletes, or teams to use their products.

Such promotional techniques are popular because the image of the products is enhanced by association with the famous people seen to be using them and the celebrities are paid to use something that they may have bought anyway. However, there are risks. Just as a product's image can be damaged by a scandal involving a celebrity, the celebrities are now being held to account for the products they promote and their own image can be damaged because of their support for something that is harmful or considered to be unethical such as the use of child labor to make soccer boots.

With so many products that are similar, companies rely heavily on advertising to convince consumers to buy their products, build brand loyalty and in some cases to pay a premium for one brand over another. However, should advertisers be allowed to do and say whatever they want?

Some people are calling for the advertising industry to be better regulated to ensure that consumers' interests are protected, especially when it comes to promoting products to children and products that may be harmful. Advertisers should be responsible for also informing consumers about known possible negative effects, for example the harm caused by cigarettes or junk food.

One argument against over-regulation though is based on the fact that it isn't against the law to sell products such as alcohol and cigarettes so why should there be restrictions on advertising them?

VOCABULARY

Here are some words that will be useful in this unit. How many do you know? Work with a partner to figure out the meaning of any words that you don't know.

ad/advertisement	consumer	lifestyle
advertiser	creativity	logo
aspire to	diversified	regulations
brand	image	sophisticated
campaign	innovative	take into account

What other words and phrases do you know related to the topic?

VOCABULARY ACTIVITIES

A. Read each definition. Fill in the blank with words from the list above.

1. promotion, plan   _____
2. new, developed using new ways of thinking   _____
3. a symbol or design used by a company   _____
4. laws or rules   _____
5. have a strong desire to have or do something   _____

B. Circle the word that best completes each sentence.

Creating the right 1. *image / innovation* is very important in advertising. Colors can have an amazing effect on us without 2. *consumers / sponsors* knowing it. But 3. *advertisers / spokespeople* are very aware of this. They know that using certain colors in 4. *a slogan / an ad* can be the difference between its success and failure. For example, in Western advertising, pink is associated with femininity whereas blue might be used more in ads for male 5. *lifestyle / image* products. Ad 6. *campaigns / innovations* that target environmentally friendly customers might use green. Red is memorable and can be emotional, as is yellow. Black and white ads can have a very 7. *sophisticated / diversified* look. A business might use blue in its 8. *brand / logo* because it's calming and professional. The next time you see an ad, check out the colors.

C. Now work with a partner. Read the paragraph aloud and compare your answers. What colors have you noticed in advertisements?

GRAPHIC ORGANIZER

Think of ads you've seen recently. How did you feel when you saw the ads? What made you remember them? In the circles, write what the ad was for, the ad's features, how you felt, etc. Then work with a partner and compare your ideas.

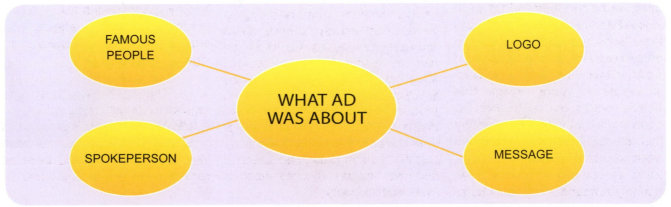

PRE-LISTENING QUESTIONS

1. Where do you notice advertisements most?
2. Do you get annoyed with a particular advert or type of advertising? Why?

SITUATION: *Mia and Kane are thinking about where to go for lunch.*

Mia	Where would you like to go for lunch?
Kane	I was given a menu and some discount vouchers for the new place on the corner. We could go there.
Mia	I wish you wouldn't always pick up those leaflets. We have so many of them now and we hardly ever look at them. It's such a waste of paper.
Kane	I don't always take them, but sometimes it's the only way to get to hear about some new places.
Mia	I'm sick of that sort of advertising; it looks so cheap. Plus, lots of people just throw them on the ground making the streets such a mess.
Kane	That's true. That reminds me, I saw something funny the other day: I picked up some rubbish by our door and you know what it was? Leaflets publicizing the 'Keep Our Town Clean' campaign. Can you believe it?
Mia	That's so funny. But doesn't it show just how bad the problem has gotten? Someone really should do something about it.
Kane	Yeah. Anyway, what about lunch? Do you want to try that café?
Mia	Not really. Anywhere that has to resort to handing out flyers and coupons to passers-by can't be very good! I prefer word-of-mouth recommendations or a review in one of my magazines.
Kane	You're such a snob. You always go for image over substance.
Mia	Hey, that's not fair!
Kane	I'm kidding. But anyway, how can you trust the reviews in those magazines? Lots of restaurants pay for them to be written so how objective do you think they are?
Mia	I don't know, but I did find out about our favorite restaurant from a magazine review. Actually, wouldn't it be nice to go there for lunch? Their food is always good and the service is good, too. Plus, I heard on the radio, they've changed their menu so you'll still get to try something new.

CHECK FOR UNDERSTANDING

1. Why doesn't Mia like leaflets?
2. What was funny about the campaign leaflet?
3. What does Kane mean by, "You always go for image over substance"?
4. What is wrong with believing a restaurant review?

Work with a partner. Compare your answers.

Quick Fact
It is estimated that $500 billion will be spent on advertisements world-wide in 2010.

PRACTICE AND DISCUSSION

PERSONALIZATION
Complete these sentences with your own ideas.

I'm not really interested in...
Wouldn't it be nice if...
I'm sick of...
I don't like how...
Wouldn't it be better if...

Now share your sentences with a classmate.

DISCUSSION STRATEGIES -
Making direct and indirect requests

There are direct and indirect ways of making requests. Imagine that you want someone to open a window:
- We are usually quite direct when we want our message to be clear.
  Example: Please open the window.
- There are other times when we prefer to communicate something without actually stating it. We refer to the desired result rather than the action itself.
  Example: Wouldn't it be nice if someone opened the window?
- Sometimes we never actually mention the action itself. It's a way of asking for something, but not in an obvious way.
  Example: It's really hot in here, isn't it?

DIRECT
Please open the window.
Could you open the window, please?
Would you mind opening the window?

INDIRECT
I could use some fresh air.
Wouldn't it be nice if someone opened the window?
Someone really should open the window.
I would love it if someone opened the window.
We'd get a nice breeze if the window was open.

Discussion Strategy in Action
Listen to the statements. Decide if the person is making a direct or indirect request.
Write down what the request is for.

1. direct / indirect   the request is for _____
2. direct / indirect   the request is for _____
3. direct / indirect   the request is for _____
4. direct / indirect   the request is for _____
5. direct / indirect   the request is for _____
6. direct / indirect   the request is for _____
7. direct / indirect   the request is for _____
8. direct / indirect   the request is for _____

Discussion Practice
Work with a partner. Take turns making direct and indirect requests for these things.

1. You are listening to someone else's radio, but it isn't loud enough.
2. You want to put up a poster for a local sports event but you can't find any tape.
3. You want to see the ads for a new job but your friend is reading the paper.

FURTHER ACTIVITIES

ROLE PLAY

1. Student A: Think about an ad you don't like. Imagine you are hired to make a new ad to replace it. Explain why you don't like the original ad and make suggestions about how you'd change it.

   Student B: You work for the company that runs the ad. Comment on the suggestions you hear. Make requests for any changes to the new ad you think are necessary.

> **Brainstorming:**
>
> What features of an ad make you really like or dislike it?
>
> Does it matter what you're advertising?
>
> What is the most important feature in an ad?
>
> Where are the most effective places to put different ads?

   What is the most successful way to advertise?
   Work with a partner. Decide on the best answers.

2. A small computer manufacturer wants to target teenagers and college kids with their new, super thin portable computer. It isn't cheap, but the company thinks that it will appeal to students. They want to concentrate on only one type of advertising (television, radio, magazines, newspapers, billboards, internet, direct mail or other). The company has come to you for advice. They have the following questions:

   • What type of advertising should they do?
   • Where should they advertise?
   • Should the advertisement concentrate more on style or information?
   • What type of advertisement should they develop – hard hitting, funny, serious, musical?
   • Should they use a celebrity?

   Compare your answers with your classmates.

ACTIVITY

Work with a partner. Read each of the product descriptions. Choose one of these products and discuss an advertising campaign for it.

Ed-U, a group of students, has just created a new, online students' magazine. It is fun, modern, and has lots of useful information for students. However, it needs lots of hits in order to keep the sponsors happy. Think of a possible advertising campaign that might attract students to the site.	**Looking Good,** a small cosmetics company, has just created a new range of men's cosmetics (moisturizer, aftershave, cleanser, etc.). They are made from organic materials and are presented very well. They are very expensive, but they last a long time.	**Hitching a Ride** is a new travel agency designed for budget travelers. The vacation packages it offers are original, fun and very cheap. Sometimes travelers might need to use local public transportation and even share rooms. This is not for people looking for a relaxing luxury holiday!

Work with another pair. Tell them what you would include in your ad campaigns.

SPEECHES - Take a stand

Imagine you are on a sports team. The team needs sponsorship money. A local restaurant says it will sponsor the team under the following conditions:

   • All of the team's shirts have the name of the restaurant on them in very large letters.
   • The team must put the restaurant's name on any posters or publicity material.
   • The players must hold all team parties at the restaurant.

Decide if you think these are reasonable conditions. Take notes. Present your recommendations.

CONSOLIDATION AND RECYCLING

BUILDING VOCABULARY

1. Work with a partner. Write synonyms for the words in the list. Try to find more than one for each word. You might need to use a dictionary.

beautiful   _____   _____

inexpensive   _____   _____

excellent   _____   _____

innovative   _____   _____

exciting   _____   _____

cool   _____   _____

funny   _____   _____

sophisticated _____   _____

2. A slogan is a short, easy to remember phrase that is used in advertising.

> *Example:*
> *An excellent way to wake up. (Coffee)*

Write slogans for three products. Use the synonyms above.

WRITING

Awards are being given to the best commercials on television worldwide.

- Imagine that you can nominate any commercial you want, past or present. Think about your favorite commercial and what makes it special. Write a persuasive letter to the judges, describing the commercial and why you think it should win.

- Read your letter to your group. Together, decide which commercial should receive the award.

Quick Fact
Tobacco companies are estimated to spend as much as US$14 million every day in advertising.

REFLECTION

1. How has this unit made you look at advertising differently?
2. How has your opinion about advertising changed during this unit?
3. What changes will be made to the way companies advertise their products in the future?

International Competitions

The latest medalists stand on a pedestal, facing their countries' flags. They are proud and will return home as heroes. But it is not just the skill and dedication of the athletes that lies behind their success; the support they have received from their country is also very important.

International rankings for sports events tend to be taken as a measure of the might of a nation and a reflection of international competition in politics and economics as much as the athletic abilities of the competitors. Therefore, many countries invest heavily in training, developing and supporting athletes. Some governments even grant citizenship to athletes from another country in order to help their medal tally and boost their nation's standing.

Few major events provide a level playing field for the competitors. Just as the world is divided along political and economic lines, there are similar divisions in sporting competitions. Sophisticated training techniques are costly and someone has to pay for them: individuals, governments, and commercial sponsors.

Wealthy, economically stable countries can and do invest much more in their athletes than poorer nations and consequently their athletes tend to do better. World-class athletes become symbols for their country and there is a lot of pressure on them to succeed at all costs. The temptation to use methods such as banned performance enhancing drugs can be too much and all too often, sportsmanship loses out to greed.

A great deal is also at stake when hosting a large international competition. Everything must run smoothly. The government and private companies make huge investments in sports facilities and infrastructure including transportation and hotel accommodation. The cost of providing security, insurance, and anti-doping measures for example have also greatly increased the cost of hosting these events.

To prepare for the 2010 FIFA World Cup, South Africa committed to improve security, renovate airports, improve the transport network, including building a high-speed rail link as well as build five new sports stadiums and refurbish others in ten cities around the country. While the South African government budgeted to spend more than $2 billion on infrastructure, policing and other needs, another $3.5 billion was promised by companies in sponsorships.

Importantly, the new infrastructure and facilities will be there for the long term and the potential returns are enormous. This means that the local population can benefit socially, politically, and economically for years to come.

The return on investment is more than dollars and cents and many organizers recognize that some form of positive discrimination is justified in the selection process to enable developing nations to host world class events. FIFA, for example, rotates the World Cup around four continents (Asia, North and South America, Europe and Africa). Others however, wonder whether developing countries like South Africa should risk this kind of investment in the first place.

VOCABULARY

Here are some words that will be useful in this unit. How many do you know? Work with a partner to figure out the meaning of any words that you don't know.

achievement	infrastructure	pride
amateur	investment	role model
anti-doping measures	level playing field	sacrifice
boycott	nationalism	unfair advantage

What other words and phrases do you know related to the topic?

VOCABULARY ACTIVITIES

A. Fill in the blanks with words from from above. Remember to use the correct word form.

1. Young athletes need to _____ their free time, friends, and social activities in order to train for international competitions.

2. Providing a good _____ of transportation, hotels, restaurants, and sports facilities is essential for the Olympic Games.

3. _____ means taking pride in your country but some people go too far.

4. Poor countries can't afford to make the big _____ now required for international competitions.

5. A country that _____ a sporting event usually refuses to go for political reasons.

B. Work with a partner. Take turns answering the questions.

1. Think of one medalist. What medal did the person get and in which event?
2. What international competitions do you like to watch?
3. Give some examples of things you compete in or compete for.
4. What has been your proudest moment?
5. What is one competitive thing you have done that has had an impact on your life?

GRAPHIC ORGANIZER

What do you think is important when determining a good international competition? Complete the chart below. Then work with a partner and compare your ideas.

	Very important	Important	Fairly important	Not important
Quality of competitors				
Facilities				
Security				
Anti-doping measures				
Transport infrastructure				
Hotels and restaurants				
Media coverage				

PRE-LISTENING QUESTIONS

1. Do you think athletes should be tested for drug use?
2. How do you think doping affects international competitions?
3. What do you think should happen to an athlete who is caught taking illegal drugs?

SITUATION: *Marcus and Lynn discuss the testing of athletes for the use of banned substances.*

Marcus	I can't believe how out of control testing athletes for doping has become! I mean athletes are treated like criminals. It's getting hard for them to compete.
Lynn	It seems to me, it's doping that's out of control. If athletes are going to do it, the authorities have to do something to control them. Otherwise, what's the point of holding competitions? Doping gives those athletes an unfair advantage.
Marcus	You could argue that lots of things give some athletes an unfair advantage, especially the richer athletes – their diet, technology, training facilities… And are drugs really any different from taking vitamins or natural supplements?
Lynn	Maybe there needs to be two different competitions, one for people who only use hard work and what nature gave them, and one for people who use drugs to do better.
Marcus	That's not a bad idea.
Lynn	I wasn't being serious.
Marcus	Yes, I know, but think about it. It's only natural that a competitor would want to do whatever it takes to win.
Lynn	No, the whole spirit of competition is to triumph against the odds – not to do something at any cost.
Marcus	Come on, think about it. There is so much pressure and money at stake. What's more, we use technology to help us every day. Doping just gives that added competitive edge.
Lynn	No, it's worse than that. And what about children, would parents want to hold up a doper as a role model? No way. Doping is bad for sports and any means of stamping it out is okay by me.

CHECK FOR UNDERSTANDING

1. What's Marcus position?
2. How does Lynn feel?
3. What does Lynn mean by "triumph against the odds" and "at any cost"?
4. Who do you agree with more, Marcus or Lynn?

Work with a partner. Compare your answers.

Quick Fact
The World Anti-Doping Agency drafted a declaration in 2005, including a strong discouragement on the use of gene doping.

PERSONALIZATION

Complete these sentences with your own ideas.

I can't believe how...

Maybe there needs to be...

It's only natural that...

We use technology to...

Now share your sentences with a classmate.

DISCUSSION STRATEGIES - Complaining

Sometimes, there is a situation we feel is unfair or we don't like. We often complain directly to the person or organization that caused the situation, for example, saying, "You shouldn't do that!" We can also complain indirectly. Here are some examples:

LESS DIRECT

MORE DIRECT

DESCRIPTION	EXAMPLES
Don't mention the offense, just that you're unhappy with the result of the offense.	You can run so fast for so long! That can't be natural.
Mention the problem in very general terms.	It's a shame that they can't run like that without drugs.
Specifically mention the offense, but do not threaten consequences.	You shouldn't use drugs to perform better!
Specifically mention the offense and be very direct about how you feel about it.	I can't stand how some athletes take drugs and think they can get away with it.
Threaten a consequence for the offense directly to the person who caused it.	Turn yourself in, or I will! It isn't fair what you're doing!
Specifically mention the offense and express your feelings in very strong terms.	I'm sick and tired of athletes not obeying the rules.

Discussion Strategy in Action

Listen to each conversation. Decide if the complaint is direct or indirect. Then write what the complaint is about.

	Direct	Indirect	What is the complaint about?
1.	☐	☐	_____
2.	☐	☐	_____
3.	☐	☐	_____
4.	☐	☐	_____
5.	☐	☐	_____

Work with a partner. Think about something in competitions that bothers you.

Take turns complaining about it.

Discussion Practice

Work with a partner. Decide the best method to use to complain about each situation.

1. The referee is making unfair calls in a game.
2. You are an athlete. You just saw one of your teammates take a banned drug.
3. The fee to participate in a marathon was raised and it's now very expensive.

FURTHER ACTIVITIES

ROLE PLAY

Work with a partner. Create a conversation for the following situation: Organizers of an international tennis circuit want to set up a big tournament in your country. It will cost a lot to prepare for and host the event.

Student A: You are a business leader. You see the tournament as a major economic opportunity. You and others in business are willing to invest some money in it, but you want the government to fund it as well. You need to convince the government.

Student B: You work for the government. You would like to see the country's scarce resources spent on developing local sports organizations and getting kids more involved in sports. Tennis is not a very popular sport in your country and is only available to a few people. You see the tennis tournament as an opportunity for big business more than anything else.

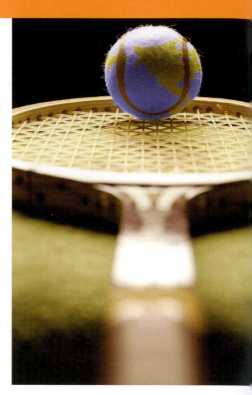

ACTIVITY

Australia	India	Thailand
Brazil	Japan	The Philippines
China	Russia	United States
England	South Korea	Other countries

Choose the top three countries which in your opinion, have done very well in international competitions. Think about the following things:

- the quality of their performances
- the style of their performances
- how well they've done in the past five years
- the kind of support they give/receive

Work with a partner. Discuss your selections and give your reasons.

Quick Fact
Around 715 million people watched the final of the 2006 FIFA World Cup™ between Italy and France.

SPEECHES - Interview

Work with a partner.

Student A: Imagine that you are going to interview a famous athlete. Ask questions and take notes. Your editor has suggested that you ask the following five questions. Think of others.
1. Why is … your favorite sport?
2. How many hours a week do you train?
3. Do you eat a special diet?
4. What do you do to prepare for a big competition?
5. What do you think makes someone a great athlete?

Student B: Pretend you are an athlete. Answer the questions as the athlete. You can use real or made-up information.

Work with another pair. Student A, present what you learned about Student B. Student B, listen and make corrections as needed.

CONSOLIDATION AND RECYCLING

BUILDING VOCABULARY

Work with a partner. Read the sentences. Pay attention to the phrasal verbs. Discuss what they mean. You might need to check some of them using a dictionary.

The runner **dropped out of** the race after he hurt his leg.

They **handed in** their registration form before the start of the race.

He **cut off** another runner on the turn and caused him to fall.

They trained hard and really **geared up** for the race.

The runner started to **run out** of steam and was passed by everyone.

Some athletes **get away with** taking drugs for a while, but most get caught in the end.

The last runner tried to **catch up** and close the gap, but remained in last place.

The referee warned the players to **watch out for** water on the field.

An athlete must be very well prepared to be **cut out for** international competition.

The players needed to **show up** for practice everyday.

You can't **count on** winning a medal at the Olympics. Most athletes won't win one.

The athlete needed to **stick with** the training program to be ready for the competition.

Take turns. Make sentences using these phrasal verbs and words from the unit to talk about international competitions.

WRITING

Describe a role model. Think of someone who you feel is a great role model for success in international competitions.

- What does the person do?
- Why do you like this person?
- What special characteristics does this person have?
- What, in particular, do you think makes this person a great role model?

Write a paragraph describing why the person is a role model. Then work with a partner. Exchange paragraphs and discuss your ideas.

REFLECTION

1. What do you think defines a successful country in terms of international competitions?
2. How important is it for a country's national identity to be good at international competitions?
3. What role does competition play in determining how a country is viewed by other countries and by its own people?

Mobile Phones

ey, WUD dis w/e? A grp of us r gunA dinA n thN 2C a moV. R U NterestD? We wr thinkN arnd 8. LMK wotU tnk n f uv a btr plan. I hope u cn cum. TTYS . BTW, I saw Gary W Cecilia D oder dy. S^ W dat???

If you can decipher all or even just parts of the message above, you are probably among the estimated two billion mobile phone users worldwide who regularly send text messages. The growing popularity of texting, also called instant messaging and SMSing (Short Message Service), has changed the way we communicate.

The size of mobile phone screens, as well as the cost of sending a message, have prompted users to include acronyms, homonyms, and abbreviations in messages, even combining letters and numbers in words to focus more on sound than spelling so for example, great becomes gr8 and later is shortened to l8tr.

People, especially teenagers, use this minimalist form of communicating to arrange social appointments, stay in contact with friends, spread gossip, send love messages, even to check the weather. Their language tends to be more casual, sometimes referred to as youth code, including

'words' such as dat fing (that thing), gonna (going to) and wanna (want to). Text messages also utilize emoticons made up of punctuation to create icons that display emotions, often representing facial expressions so shocked, sleepy, and crying become (O_O), (~.~) and (;_;).

This kind of language is also commonly used in emails and Internet chat rooms, but there is even more shortening of words when used on a phone. Text messaging, as a medium of communication, has grown so much and become so natural that in 2003 a 13-year-old girl in Scotland wrote a short essay using only SMS shorthand. Reports of this set off a major controversy over whether it is appropriate to use these forms of words in schools and their effect on the English language: whether it increases errors in spelling and punctuation and leads to fewer complete sentences. Many educators are concerned that students won't know how to use their native language properly if the trend continues. The

controversy intensified in 2006 when the Scottish Qualifications Authority, which sets testing standards in Scotland, announced that phrases like *2B R NT 2B* (to be or not to be) and *I LUV U* would be accepted in exam papers.

Thousands of miles away in New Zealand, a similar decision by education officials there to tolerate abbreviations like *wot* (what), *wanna* and *cuz* (because) prompted one member of parliament to protest, writing that "skoolz r ther 2 educ8 + raze litracy 2 certn standrds" (schools are there to educate and raise literacy to certain standards).

There is a concern that as students graduate and join the workforce, they will be at a disadvantage because of their inability to know when it is and is not appropriate to use the new abbreviated word forms. However, others argue that it is the older workers who may feel alienated as technology continues to affect the way we communicate.

VOCABULARY

Here are some words that will be useful in this unit. How many do you know? Work with a partner to figure out the meaning of any words that you don't know.

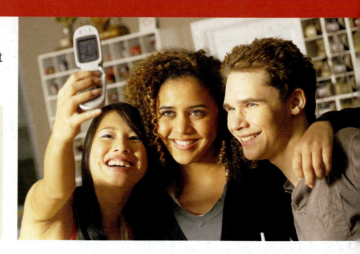

abbreviate	essential	set off
affect	in close contact	set up
bullying	minimalist	text message
decipher	popularity	trend
enact	representing	turn off

What other words and phrases do you know related to the topic?

VOCABULARY ACTIVITIES

A. Synonyms are words that are the same or similar in meaning. Look at the words below. Find a synonym in the list above.

SMS   **shut off**   **necessary**   **harassing**   **arrange**

B. Read each sentence. Replace the underlined word with a synonym.

1. The government <u>passed</u> a law about using mobile phones while driving.
2. Her essay <u>caused</u> a controversy in the school.
3. He <u>shortened</u> see you to CU.
4. Mobile phones have had a big <u>influence</u> on how we communicate.
5. The man doesn't text message so he couldn't <u>figure out</u> the message from his son.

C. Work with a partner. Write an SMS. Your partner will decipher it.

GRAPHIC ORGANIZER

Think about the things you do every day. How much do you use technology? Fill in the chart below. Then work with a partner and compare your ideas.

ACTIVITY	HOURS / DAY	REASON
Internet		
TV		
Mobile phone calls		
Text messaging		
Study		
Sleep		
Eat		
Class		
Video games		
Other		

PRE-LISTENING QUESTIONS

1. Do you think a mobile phone is essential in today's society?
2. What are some advantages and disadvantages of having a mobile phone?
3. What would you do if your phone was lost or stolen?

SITUATION: *Jacob has lost his mobile phone.*

Jacob I am going absolutely crazy without my mobile phone! It's been three days and I still haven't found it. It's my lifeline.

Amy You're kidding. I don't know why you are so dependent on it. I don't have a mobile phone and I do just fine. I actually enjoy the fact that people can't contact me anytime, anywhere.

Jacob You don't understand. My phone is how I wake up in the morning, check the time and the news, how I set up meetings with friends. It's how I run my life.

Amy But you can contact people using the phone at home or a pay phone or you can email, can't you? What's the big deal?

Jacob Yeah, well, I got rid of the phone at home because I wasn't using it and email is such a pain. It's just so much simpler to use a mobile phone. Once you get used to it, it's hard to go back.

Amy That's partly why I never got a mobile; I didn't want to become reliant on it. It's like an addiction for some people. It's so rude when I'm talking to a friend and they answer their phone without even saying, "excuse me." It's like they can't wait to talk to someone else.

Jacob Uh huh, but not everyone does that.

Amy Okay, or how about if some friends come over to watch a DVD and they sit there text messaging other people. It feels like they don't really want to spend time with me. Or when I'm sitting in a restaurant, I really don't want to hear the person next to me talking about his or her problems.

Jacob Right, that's rude. You should just say something though. Look, you have some valid points; some people are inconsiderate, but that's just the way it is. For me, the advantages far outweigh the disadvantages. Amy, you'll get one soon, I bet.

Amy You're probably right. Well, anyway, I hope find your phone soon!

CHECK FOR UNDERSTANDING

1. Why is Jacob upset?
2. Why does he say his phone is his lifeline?
3. Why does Amy object to mobile phones?
4. Do you think she'll change her mind after talking to Jacob?
5. Who do you agree with more, Jacob or Amy? Give reasons.

Work with a partner. Compare your answers.

Quick Fact
Ministry of Information Industry figures show that 480 million people owned a mobile phone in China in 2007.

PRACTICE AND DISCUSSION

PERSONALIZATION

Complete these sentences with your own ideas.

I enjoy the fact that…
My phone is how I…
I think it's so rude when…
I don't want to hear the person next to me…
Just because the technology exists, doesn't mean people have to…

Now share your sentences with a classmate.

Quick Fact
It is estimated that less than 20% of all unused mobile phones in the UK are recycled

DISCUSSION STRATEGIES - Showing that you are listening

Sometimes, we want to let a speaker know we are actively listening and following what's being said but without interrupting. Some ways we do this are: nodding our head, smiling, gesturing, and uttering short phrases. Some phrases/utterances to use are:

AGREEMENT	SURPRISE / DISBELIEF
Uh huh	Really
Um hmm	No way
Yeah	You're kidding
Sounds good	Oh no
Okay	Wow
Right	

Discussion Strategy in Action

Listen to the following conversations. Is the other person really listening to the speaker? How can you tell?

1. _____
2. _____
3. _____

Work with a partner. Practice one of the conversations.

Discussion Practice

Conduct a survey about phone use amongst your classmates. Take turns presenting your survey results to your partner. Discuss your ideas. Use the discussion strategies to show that you are listening. Consider:

- when it's okay to use a mobile phone
- how often classmates text message
- what new features classmates would like to have on their mobile phones

Brainstorming:

How often do you call your friends?

What kind of things do you talk about on the phone?

How often do you send pictures or text messages?

FURTHER ACTIVITIES

ROLE PLAY

Work with a partner. Create phone conversations and text messages.

1. Two people are making plans to do something together on Saturday night. One of them likes quiet activities, but the other one wants to do something more active, like go clubbing.

2. Two friends are talking. One of them has a big problem at work and needs some advice.

3. Two friends are talking about a problem that came up over the weekend with a boyfriend/girlfriend. One of them is upset and the other is listening and offering advice.

4. A man has been offered a job in another city. It is a great opportunity for him, but he won't get to see his girlfriend as often. They come up with different ways to stay in touch.

ACTIVITY

Work with a partner or in a small group. Imagine that you work for a company that manufactures mobile phones. You want to produce a new range of phones that will appeal to as many different types of users as possible, from the person who just has a phone for emergencies to the person who uses it all the time.

Provide descriptions of five mobile phones. How much would you be able to charge for each one?

Compare your phones with other groups. How many people in your class would buy one of your phones?

> **Brainstorming:**
>
> How big and how heavy would the phone be?
> What features would you include?
> What makes your most expensive phone special?
> How many of each model would you make?
> What type of user would buy each model?

SPEECHES - Here's what I'd say

Discuss the situations listed below with a partner. What would you say or do in each situation?

1. You are having dinner with a friend you haven't seen in a long time. You had been looking forward to dinner with her. You friend keeps taking messages on her mobile. How do you react?

2. You are in the library trying to study. Someone keeps receiving calls. You can hear the conversations, making it hard for you to concentrate. How do you react?

3. You are at a movie theater and several people sitting near you keep calling their friends to tell them what's happening in the movie. How do you react?

4. You sent some photos to a friend on your mobile. Your friend sent them on to a lot of people. You weren't expecting this to happen and you are not happy. What do you say?

5. You work for a bus company. You've been asked to come up with a courtesy campaign for use of mobile phones. What would you include?

CONSOLIDATION AND RECYCLING

BUILDING VOCABULARY

Create a survey about mobile phone and text messaging attitudes and habits. Use vocabulary from this and previous units. Ask five classmates to take the survey.

Include at least eight questions, such as:

1. Where and when do you use your mobile phone most frequently?
2. How often do you text message?
3. To whom do you send messages most frequently?
4. If you could add new features to your mobile, what would they be?

Quick Fact
Mobile phones can take videos, but now, many media companies are producing short videos to be watched on mobile phones.

Take turns presenting your survey results to the class. Discuss your ideas. Can you make any conclusions about:

• when it's okay to use a mobile phone?

• how often classmates text message?

• what new features classmates would like to have on their mobile phones?

WRITING

Some people think schools should make restrictions on phones and text messaging.

Write a short newspaper article about why you think schools should or should not make restrictions on phones and text messaging. Include reasons and examples to support the position you take.

Form groups. Take turns reading each other's articles. Compare ideas and reasons.

REFLECTION

1. How have your opinions about mobile phones and text messaging changed over the course of this unit?
2. Why are mobile phones and text messaging such an integral part of society now?
3. What impact have mobile phones, text messaging, and other technology had on daily life?

Manners & Etiquette

Mr. Ito hands Mr. Reynolds his business card. Mr. Reynolds doesn't look at it and just puts it in his pocket. Mr. Reynolds then walks into the restaurant, not noticing that everyone else has removed their shoes and put on slippers. This is Mr. Reynolds's first time in Japan and he isn't off to a very good start.

Manners and etiquette are the rules that a society says we should follow. They govern everything from what we say to what we wear. The problem is, the rules aren't the same all over the world and that can lead to some very embarrassing situations. To try and minimize offensive behavior, many books have been written as guidelines for how to act properly in different countries. Here are excerpts from a book giving information for travelers to Brazil:

Greetings
Saying hello and goodbye is very important; everyone present should be greeted and bid farewell personally. To miss someone would be inconsiderate. Women greet everyone with a kiss on each cheek unless they are single, in which case after kissing each cheek once, they will kiss the first cheek again. Friends and family will meet with an embrace - even men.

Conversation
People stand really close when speaking to each other. It is also acceptable to touch the other person with a hand on their shoulder, back, or arm. In fact, backing away could be an insult. Eye contact is respectful unless it is with someone of higher rank. During a conversation, people will interrupt, talk over each other, and raise their voices. This is not considered rude, but passionate.

Timeliness
Normally people arrive ten to fifteen minutes late, or even half an hour or more. The higher a person's status, the later they can be - the better to make an entrance. Arriving on time is neither common nor expected, but it is polite and courteous.

Dress
Women and men tend to be stylish at all times. People dress to impress and sloppy appearance is generally unacceptable.

Dining
Meals may be very long and very social. When eating, keep both hands above the table. The knife is usually held in the left hand and the fork in the right. It would be a faux pas to touch any food, including fruit, with your hands. Drinks are always poured into glasses, never drunk from a bottle. Finally, try to eat all of whatever is put in front of you, no matter how bad or how much. It is rude to turn your nose up to what is offered as it means you disapprove not only of the food but also of the person who served it. It's best to just try to appreciate it.

Gift Giving
Gifts are given by guests when visiting another's home. The gifts should be thoughtful, but not overly generous, especially in business relationships as they may be interpreted as a bribe. In Brazil, one is supposed to open a gift immediately upon receiving it, in front of the 'giver' and comment there and then on the gift; to not do so could offend the gift-giver.

How would the information in a guidebook about your country compare with this?

VOCABULARY

Here are some words that will be useful in this unit. How many do you know? Work with a partner to figure out the meaning of any words that you don't know.

acceptable	guidelines	respectful
appreciate	impress	rude
bid farewell	inconsiderate	sloppy
courteous	insult	taboo
disapprove	offensive	thoughtful
embarrassing	polite	turn your nose up
faux pas	properly	unacceptable

What other words and phrases do you know related to the topic?

VOCABULARY ACTIVITIES

A. Categorize the words in the list above. Can you add any more words related to manners and etiquette?

Positive	Neutral	Negative
_____	_____	_____
_____	_____	_____
_____	_____	_____
_____	_____	_____
_____	_____	_____
_____	_____	_____

B. Work with a partner. Think about your own culture. Answer the questions.

1. What do your grandparents disapprove of you doing?
2. How many examples of an offensive gesture can you think of?
3. What is a major faux pas at the dinner table?
4. What is considered polite and courteous regarding keeping to an appointment?
5. Imagine you work in a large company and someone has given your boss an expensive bottle of wine. Would it impress, embarrass, or upset your boss? Why?

GRAPHIC ORGANIZER

What is considered bad manners? What is considered good manners?
Think about your own country or another country you know about. Fill in the chart below.
Then work with a partner and compare your ideas.

GOOD MANNERS	BAD MANNERS

PRE-LISTENING QUESTIONS

1. Do you have concerns about traveling far from home?
2. What is the furthest you've traveled?
3. What are some of the biggest challenges faced when traveling?

SITUATION: *Lara is nervous about her business trip.*

Lara Hey, Sam! I'm going to be going on a business trip to Malaysia next month. You were there last year, right?

Sam Yeah, it's a great place, so different to here.

Lara I was wondering if you'd be willing to give me some advice on what to expect and how to behave there. I'm worried about making a major faux pas and embarrassing myself.

Sam That's silly. There's no need to be embarrassed about making a mistake and anyway most of my best travel stories are the result of finding myself in an unfamiliar situation.

Lara Maybe... but I really don't want to do anything offensive. I'd feel terrible if I did. So could you possibly give me some tips and guidelines?

Sam Sure. You've heard the expression, 'when in Rome, do as the Romans do,' haven't you? Just keep your eyes open, pay attention to what people do and follow their lead.

Lara Yeah, but I don't want to just copy others and I certainly don't want to come across as rude or inconsiderate.

Sam You worry too much.

Lara But, what if I do something really unacceptable?

Sam Listen. They'll know you are a foreigner and won't expect you to be exactly like them. I think as long as you make an effort, people will understand and appreciate it. Just remember, if there's something you're uncomfortable with try not to show it. They might think you disapprove of their culture. And don't turn your nose up at food without trying it. That kind of thing is pretty easy to remember. It's only the seriously taboo things you need to be really careful about, like wearing skimpy clothing or offering someone alcohol because that could definitely be offensive.

Lara I am looking forward to the trip; I want it to go well so that my boss lets me travel overseas more.

Sam Look. I have a booklet on what's acceptable in Malaysia. I'll give it to you tomorrow.

✔ CHECK FOR UNDERSTANDING

1. What is Lara worried about?
2. What does Sam say to reassure her?
3. What are two taboos Sam mentions?
4. Do you think Sam has traveled a lot? Give reasons.

Work with a partner. Compare your answers.

Quick Fact
In Malaysia, only the right hand is used for eating.

PRACTICE AND DISCUSSION

PERSONALIZATION

Complete these sentences with your own ideas.

> *I'm really nervous about...*
> *I'm worried I'm going to...*
> *I'd feel terrible if...*
> *I don't want to come across as...*
> *As long as you make an effort, people will...*

Now share your sentences with a classmate.

DISCUSSION STRATEGIES - Making requests

When we want someone to do something, we make a polite request. A simple request starting or ending with "please" can be used in most contexts *("Please open the window.")*. Sometimes we may want to be more formal.

MORE FORMAL

LESS FORMAL

I was wondering if you'd be willing to...
Would you mind ____ing...?
Could you possibly...?
Could you (please) do me a favor and...?
Would you (please)...?
Please...
..., please.

Quick Fact
Chopsticks should be held in the right hand, even by people who are left-handed.

Discussion Strategy in Action

Listen carefully to the requests. Circle one letter to show how formal each request is. A is more formal and D is less formal. Then write down what is being requested.

Formality   What is being requested?

1. A   B   C   D   _____

2. A   B   C   D   _____

3. A   B   C   D   _____

4. A   B   C   D   _____

5. A   B   C   D   _____

Discussion Practice

Work with a partner. Take turns making formal and informal requests.

Example:
Could you let me use your dictionary for a minute?

FURTHER ACTIVITIES

ROLE PLAY

Work with a partner. Create a short conversation for each of the situations.

1. Someone is smoking near you and the smoke is blowing in your face. What would you say? Would it matter if the person is: bigger than you/your boss/your friend's father?

2. Your friend often calls you late at night even though he/she knows that you go to bed early. What would you say? Would it be different if it was: someone you loved/someone with a serious problem/someone trying to sell you something?

3. You are in a movie theater. The person next to you keeps calling a friend. She is speaking loudly.

4. You are at an important dinner and there are dishes you don't want to try. The host is serving the best dishes from his country. They are difficult to prepare and are very expensive.

> **Brainstorming:**
> What are some things that people do that you consider rude?
>
> What would you say to someone who is doing something rude?
>
> When is it better to just ignore someone who is being rude?

ACTIVITY

GUIDE TO INTERNATIONAL GIFT GIVING

Australia - One thing that may be inappropriate is giving wine from another country (unless you brought it from that country yourself) - there is lots of excellent wine there already.

France - Gifts needn't be expensive, but should be of good quality. People may be offended by an inferior gift. If giving flowers, avoid giving odd numbers, especially 13. People rarely count the number, but historically it was considered unlucky. The number of flowers given to a lover is often 6 or 12 and should therefore be avoided otherwise.

Korea - Gifts should not be overly expensive as the receiver will feel like they must give a gift of equal value. One should not give sharp objects like knives or scissors (symbols of severing a relationship), green headwear, or objects with red lettering (it usually means death). Four is also avoided as it is a number associated with death.

The United States - There are no real taboos on gift giving. Flowers or candy are often given by dinner guests. Alcohol may be given, but generally only if the guest knows the host drinks alcohol.

Vietnam - Handkerchiefs symbolize a sad farewell and so shouldn't be given. However, things used in daily life, such as useful objects and decorations or special soaps, are appreciated. Gifts for children are also welcomed.

Imagine that you will be going to the following countries. What gifts from your own country would you take for people you meet in each country?

Australia _____   The United States _____   Korea _____

France _____   Vietnam _____

If some people were coming to your country, what advice would you give them about giving gifts?

SPEECHES - A lesson

Work with a partner. You are teaching a group of business people about the way to behave in your country or a country you know well. Pick two of the following topics and one more subject that you think will interest the businessmen. Prepare your lesson.

Greetings	Timeliness	Dress Codes
Conversation	Dining	Gift Giving

Form groups. Take turns presenting your lessons.

CONSOLIDATION AND RECYCLING

BUILDING VOCABULARY

Un-, in-, im- and *dis-* are all prefixes and when they are added to some adjectives they create the opposite meaning. Read the sentences below and fill in the blanks with the more appropriate words.

1. In Ecuador, it is (*polite/impolite*) _____ to yawn in public, so you shouldn't do it.
2. It is usually considered (*inappropriate/appropriate*) _____ to touch or stay close to someone from Finland. They like more personal space and expect the space around them to be (*respected/disrespected*) _____ .
3. Be (*discourteous/courteous*) _____ in Hong Kong by using a person's family name until specifically told to use their given name.
4. Canadians are (*impressed/unimpressed*) _____ with people who compare their country with the United States. In fact, they may be upset and find it a bit (*offensive/inoffensive*) _____ .
5. While Mexicans think being 30 minutes late is okay for themselves, they (*approve/disapprove*) _____ of foreign visitors being late.

Work with a partner. Review the adjectives from this unit and earlier units. Make a list of adjectives that can take the negative prefixes above.

Example:
acceptable / unacceptable

WRITING

Write an advice column in a newspaper for each of the following situations. The advice for each situation should be given in no more than 50 words. Be as thorough as possible, including everything you can think of that might be important.

1. Advice for someone attending a job interview.
2. Advice for someone getting their first mobile phone.
3. Advice for someone meeting their boyfriend's/girlfriend's parents for the first time over dinner.

Present your ideas to a partner or small group.

REFLECTION

1. What is the best way to learn about the manners and etiquette of another country?
2. What are some things that might be considered rude anywhere in the world?
3. How tolerant of untypical behavior are you?

Volunteering

Helping others is often considered a moral obligation. However, in some cultures, any sense of compulsion raises questions about the sincerity of the volunteers' acts.

How individuals and societies look upon voluntary service is based on a combination of factors such as history, culture, government and religion. In Cambodia, volunteerism has traditionally been fostered by respected monks and village elders who would lead people to work together. This is reflected in a Cambodian phrase, *nak smak chet*, meaning to work with a sincere heart without payment or any benefit.

Volunteering and performing charitable acts in general usually focus on kindness to others, often through personal relationships. In China for example, people commonly feel tied together by a network of family and community through a system of *guanxi* (personal connections) which is based on beliefs in compassion, righteousness, and loyalty.

Voluntary acts of kindness are encouraged in towns and cities, but they are especially important in more remote areas. In rural parts of Indonesia for example, all members of the community, young and old, participate in building homes, roads and bridges as well as working the land and joining preparations for weddings, funerals, and religious festivals. This is called *gotong royong*, meaning mutual assistance.

Traditional proverbs and folk songs commonly demonstrate the responsibility people feel towards their community and to assisting one another. 'The healthy leaf covers the torn' is an example of a Vietnamese proverb that reflects the sense of mutual support which has helped the Vietnamese, a nation of people who have traditionally relied heavily on farming to survive hardships such as unpredictable weather.

Volunteering is still important today. In China, Lei Feng is held up as a modern role model. Lei Feng died in 1962 and though he was only 22 when he died, he had devoted himself to practicing selfless acts for others. He is even featured in a popular video game where the players advance to the next level only after completing a number of charitable acts, performing such ordinary things as mending a person's socks.

People around the world volunteer for community activities such as helping out at hospitals and at boys' and girls' clubs. In the United States, this sense of civic duty is being promoted in the educational system with more and more schools now requiring students to do some charitable work in order to graduate.

Educators want students to be exposed to these kinds of experiences so that they will be more likely to continue to volunteer as adults. Although participation in community service is mandatory, many students find it rewarding and undertake it willingly. They feel they are part of a community and that they can make a difference in the lives of others.

VOCABULARY

Here are some words that will be useful in this unit. How many do you know? Work with a partner to figure out the meaning of any words that you don't know.

assist	promote	sincere
charitable	selfless	volunteer
benefit	moral obligation	civic duty
loyalty	mutual	community service
tradition	reflected in	mandatory
devoted	respected	rewarding

What other words and phrases do you know related to the topic?

VOCABULARY ACTIVITIES

A. Antonyms are words that have opposite meanings. Work with a partner. For each word below, find its antonym from the list above.

selfish voluntary harm unfulfilling not honest or true

B. Discuss the following questions.

1. What types of civic duties would you like to perform?
2. Which charities do people contribute to in your community?
3. What are some of the benefits of volunteering?
4. Why don't more people volunteer?

> **Quick Fact**
> According to the 2000 National Survey on Individual Giving, Pakistanis have at 58 percent one of the highest rates of volunteering in the world.

GRAPHIC ORGANIZER

"Give a man a fish and he eats for a day. Teach a man to fish and he eats for a lifetime"
— a well-known proverb

List different ways of helping people, animals, or the environment. Then work with a partner and compare your ideas. Discuss which of your ideas will benefit the most people, have a longer impact, and be the most useful?

IDEA	BENEFIT	IMPACT

POINTS OF VIEW *I've got more important things to do.*

PRE-LISTENING QUESTIONS

1. Do you think it is a good idea for schools to make community service mandatory?
2. Would you support this type of volunteering? Why?

SITUATION: *Ray thinks volunteering is a waste of his time.*

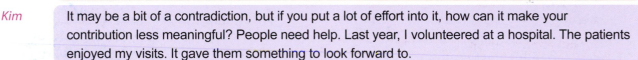

Ray	My university is now insisting that we do some voluntary service or we can't graduate. I'm trying to finish my course and look for a job; I really don't have time for it.
Kim	Don't you think you are being a bit selfish, Ray? It's only what, 2 or 3 hours a week, right? We should help other people. It is our responsibility.
Ray	Don't get me wrong, I agree, in principle. It's just that I think it's more important to choose to help and not be told I have to. How can it be voluntary if it is mandatory? It's a contradiction and it makes our contribution less meaningful, doesn't it?
Kim	It may be a bit of a contradiction, but if you put a lot of effort into it, how can it make your contribution less meaningful? People need help. Last year, I volunteered at a hospital. The patients enjoyed my visits. It gave them something to look forward to.
Ray	Well, the students I work with don't look forward to me coming to help them. I'm tutoring at an elementary school. The students aren't interested in learning; they won't even try. It's a total waste of time. How do you help people who don't want your help?
Kim	Maybe they sense that you don't want to be there; that you only come because you have to. Try a different approach. Try to get to know them. Figure out what they need your help with. Forget that it's something you have to do.
Ray	Good points. I know there are benefits for me, too. I'm building some job skills and getting some work experience.
Kim	Exactly. It's a win-win situation. When I started volunteering at the hospital, it was really tough, but I gradually got to know the patients and looked forward to going every week. I still volunteer there from time to time. I'm glad that my school required us to volunteer. I also learned skills that helped me get my job.
Ray	Yeah, I'll try to look at things differently and if tutoring doesn't work out, I could always try to help out in other ways. Thanks for your help, it's good to have someone like you to talk to.
Kim	No problem. Stay with it; you'll see that it's worth it.

CHECK FOR UNDERSTANDING

1. Is Ray for or against mandatory volunteering? How can you tell?
2. Why does Kim think it is our duty to volunteer?
3. What does Kim recommend that Ray do?
4. Do you agree with her advice?
5. How would you summarize each person's point of view?

Work with a partner. Compare your answers.

Quick Fact
2001 was designated International Year of the Volunteer by the United Nations.

PERSONALIZATION

Complete these sentences with your own ideas.

I don't have time to…

I would really like to help…

It might be a good idea to…

I need to change my attitude toward…

Now share your sentences with a classmate.

DISCUSSION STRATEGIES – Offering to help

There are many ways we can express a desire to help others. Of the phrases listed below, which are formal and which are informal?

Hey, do you need some help?

Can I help you?

Would you like any help _____ing?

I'd be glad to help you _____ if you'd like.

I would like to offer my help.

Let me give you a hand.

I'd be happy to help out.

Please let me know if I can be of further assistance.

Quick Fact
Australians volunteer 836 million hours per year which contributes an estimated $42 billion a year to the Australian economy.

Discussion Strategy in Action

Listen to each conversation. Decide if the offer to help is formal or informal.

1. formal / informal

2. formal / informal

3. formal / informal

4. formal / informal

Quick Fact
In the US, more women participated in volunteering than men across all education and age levels, marital and employment status and race.

Discussion Practice

A local organization is arranging a summer program in a school in a third world country.

Work with a partner. You want to help arrange the program and also want to work in the school. Think of the skills you have, the subjects you could teach, or other ways you can help. Think of different ways of offering to help the organization, the teachers, and the students.

FURTHER ACTIVITIES

ROLE PLAY

Work with a partner. Create a conversation for the following situations.

1. Your local library needs volunteers to read stories to young children on Saturday mornings. You talk to the librarian about volunteering.

2. You notice that it's getting harder for your grandparents to do their daily activities. They are very independent. You talk to one of them to offer to help out in the evening.

3. You heard that a local club is having a fun run to raise money for an arts center. You want to help with the publicity. You talk to a member of the club about making posters to put up around town and designing ads for the local newspaper. What other ways could you help?

ACTIVITY

Work with a partner or in a small group. Think about your community. What could you do to make it a better place to live?

Brainstorm some ideas. Then decide on a volunteer project. Discuss the details. Take notes.

> **Quick Fact**
> April is National Volunteer Month in the US while in the Philippines and Singapore it is National Volunteer Month in December.

Examples of possible projects:
- creating a play area for young children
- building a skate park for older kids
- making audio recordings of books for people who cannot see well enough to read
- planting flowers make parts of the town more attractive

Present your project to your classmates.

SPEECHES - Ask for support

Work with a partner. Imagine you have organized a homework club. Some local high school students have volunteered to help younger students with their homework after school. They will meet twice a week. The volunteers won't be paid, but you need some supplies for the program. You need school supplies such as paper, pencils, and calculators. You would also like to give the younger students snacks.

You decide to talk to the owner of a local business to explain your program and ask for money to buy supplies or for a donation of supplies. Organize your presentation. Include information about your volunteer program and what you need.

Work with another pair. Take turns giving your presentations.

BUILDING VOCABULARY

By learning to recognize the common roots of words along with prefixes and suffixes you will increase your vocabulary and improve your ability to understand new words.

bene- is the root of words meaning well or favorable

benefit   benevolence   benefactor

communis- is the root of words meaning public or general

community   communicate   communal

pop- is the root of words meaning people

popular   population   populous

Now write five sentences using these words.
Find more common roots from other words from this or earlier units.
Share your sentences and the roots of different words with a partner.

Quick Fact
In West Bengal, India, volunteers give, on average, 23.5 hours of service per month with 75% coming from rural areas.

WRITING

Work with a partner. Think of a volunteer organization, it could be real or imaginary.
Write a newspaper article about its work. Include:

- its aims i.e. who or what it helps
- what is involved
- where and when the volunteer activity takes place
- any special skills the volunteers need
- other information about the organization

Quick Fact
Only one in every four people in Canada volunteer, and 75% of all hours of volunteer work come from less then 10% of the total Canadian population.

REFLECTION

1. What is volunteering?
2. How have you changed your view about volunteering from the beginning of the unit?
3. Are you more or less likely to volunteer now?

8

Health and Nature

With our busy lives convenience is important, but are we sacrificing our health and the environment for quick fixes? How conscious of our affect on our health and the environment are you? Answer the questions below to find out.

1 **Air quality** in our homes is a big issue. Pollutants from the environment can get into our homes. However, keeping houseplants is an easy and natural way of filtering them out of the air. How many plants do you have in your house?

   a. none   b. one or two   c. three or more

2 **Driving a car** creates pollution and probably adds to global warming; both of which are bad for our long-term health. Try to drive less and use public transport more. Even better, walk or ride a bicycle and benefit from the extra exercise as well. How often do you drive a car?

   a. usually   b. occasionally   c. never

3 **Refined foods**, such as white flour and rice, have the vitamins and minerals taken out (although sometimes they are then artificially put back). These foods are often quick and convenient, but are they the healthiest choice? How often do you eat refined foods?

   a. very often or always   b. once in a while

   c. never

4 **Foods grown using pesticides** can harm your health. Organic foods are usually more expensive, but they are generally considered to be safer. How often do you eat organic foods?

   a. never   b. once in a while

   c. very often or always

5 **Importing foods** can be more costly and creates pollution. It also often means that the food is not as fresh as food grown nearby. How often do you check where your food has come from?

   a. never   b. once in a while

   c. very often or always

6 **Cleaning products** might make your house shine, but they can be toxic, some may even cause health problems. You can replace most chemical cleaners with more natural alternatives such as vinegar and baking soda. How often do you use chemical cleaners?

   a. very often or always

   b. once in a while   c. never

What's your Natural Health Check score?
Add up your score: a=0 points, b=1 point, c=2 points

If you scored...	
0 - 5 points	You should think about the longer term consequences for your health and the environment. A few small changes would go a long way to improving things!
6 - 10 points	You are already doing quite a lot to look after your health and the environment, but look at other possible improvements.
11 - 14 points	You are trying to achieve a healthy lifestyle on a number of fronts. Excellent. Give yourself a pat on the back and keep up the good work!

VOCABULARY

Here are some words that will be useful in this unit. How many do you know? Work with a partner to figure out the meaning of any words that you don't know.

alternatives	houseplant	organic
chemicals	imported	pesticides
consequences	local	pollution
exercise	long-term	toxic
global warming	minerals	vitamins

What other words and phrases do you know related to the topic?

VOCABULARY ACTIVITIES

A. Complete the sentences with words from the list above. Remember to use the correct word form. Work with a partner. Compare your answers and discuss the statements, do you agree with them?

  1. Without enough _____ and minerals, our bodies can't function properly.

  2. _____ are added to some products so they work well and smell pleasant.

  3. _____ products do not contain _____ , but tend to be more expensive.

  4. When buying food it is important to consider if it's _____ or grown locally.

  5. Riding a bike provides good _____ and reduces _____ that would have been created from driving a car.

B. Fill in the blanks in the chart with the correct forms of the words.

NOUN	VERB	ADJECTIVE
		digestive
	disinfect	
		poisonous

NOUN	VERB	ADJECTIVE
		refined
	filter	
	pollute	

GRAPHIC ORGANIZER

What are some ways to be healthy? List your ideas. Then work with a partner and compare your ideas.

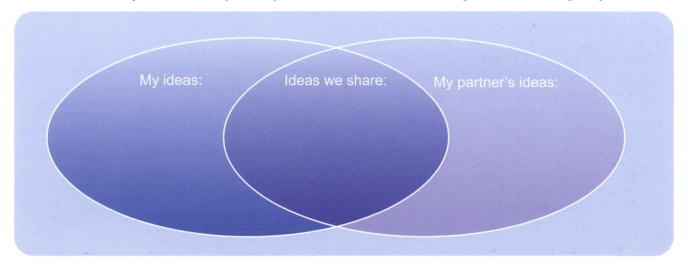

My ideas:

Ideas we share:

My partner's ideas:

PRE-LISTENING QUESTIONS

1. How much do you spend on shampoo, soap, and other personal care products?
2. How do you decide what kind of personal care products you're going to buy?

SITUATION: *Lara and Julie are discussing a new store at the mall.*

Lara	There's a new natural cosmetics store at the mall and…
Julie	You mean the one that uses those blue bottles?
Lara	Well, actually they're green, but yes; anyway, the store is fabulous and…
Julie	Sorry for interrupting you again, but I stopped by that store recently and I think their stuff is overpriced and overrated.
Lara	I don't know why you would say that. The prices are only a little higher and...
Julie	Please! A little higher? They're twice the price. And I can't stand the way they play on the 'green shopper' stuff so much when in fact just because something is made with natural ingredients doesn't mean it's safe. Natural products can be toxic, too.
Lara	Hold on, I think you're missing the point. Their products use organic ingredients that are better for the environment. If consumers start demanding more organic products, it'll make a real difference and…
Julie	Oh come on, I really doubt that by buying overpriced cosmetics it's going to have much impact. The products aren't even very good. I tried some so-called natural shampoo once. It was awful. I'll stick to products that work best.
Lara	Some natural products might not be as good, but that doesn't mean all are bad. The same can be said for ordinary products, too. I mean, some products are just better than others, right? You can't say something is bad just because it's natural and made from…
Julie	Sure, but can I just say, I think a lot of companies are cashing in on consumers wanting to help the planet. Words like, 'natural', 'organic', and 'green' are on so many new products now and I don't see that they're any better. It's just a way to increase profits.
Lara	I don't know why you're so hostile. Personally, I get great satisfaction in knowing that when I buy a product, I'm not hurting the planet or myself. We all have to play our part…
Julie	That's just it though. I'm tired of being made to feel ashamed for not buying organic things when I can't afford them and don't think they're as good anyway.
Lara	I'm sorry. I just wanted to tell you about a new store, that was all.

CHECK FOR UNDERSTANDING

1. What are Lara's reasons for buying natural products?
2. What are Julie's reasons for not buying natural products?
3. Do you agree with either of them? Why?

Work with a partner. Compare your answers.

Quick Fact
Cornstarch can be used to clean windows and carpets, and also to polish furniture.

PRACTICE AND DISCUSSION

PERSONALIZATION

Complete these sentences with your own ideas.

I really think…

I get great satisfaction in knowing…

I can't afford to spend so much for….

If consumers…

I can't stand the way…

Now share your sentences with a classmate.

DISCUSSION STRATEGIES - Interrupting

Sometimes we need to interrupt another person while they are speaking. We may want to clarify a point, ask a question, make a point, or to abruptly end a conversation. It is important to make interruptions as polite as possible though. Some examples are:

Hold on…

Sorry to interrupt, but...

Can I (just) say…

Right, and you know that…

I need to add something here.

May I say something?

Excuse me...

I'm sorry, but…

Quick Fact
Eastern medicine is often considered the "natural" alternative to Western medicine.

Discussion Strategy in Action

Listen. For each conversation, check the box that best explains why the person interrupted.

1. ☐ a. clarify a point
   ☐ b. ask a question
   ☐ c. make a point
   ☐ d. end the conversation

2. ☐ a. clarify a point
   ☐ b. ask a question
   ☐ c. make a point
   ☐ d. end the conversation

3. ☐ a. clarify a point
   ☐ b. ask a question
   ☐ c. make a point
   ☐ d. end the conversation

4. ☐ a. clarify a point
   ☐ b. ask a question
   ☐ c. make a point
   ☐ d. end the conversation

Discussion Practice

Work with a partner. Discuss the topics below. Practice interrupting your partner to clarify a point, ask a question, and so on.

- eating organic food
- eating fast food and convenience food
- using natural remedies for a cold

FURTHER ACTIVITIES

ROLE PLAY

Work with a partner. Imagine that you and some friends are moving into a new house. You will share all the expenses equally and take turns to do the shopping and cooking. There is almost no food and no cleaning products. You also want to buy some furniture.

Student A: You are very careful about what you buy. You eat healthily and exercise regularly. You are concerned about spending too much but would prefer to spend a little more if it is better for your health or the environment.

Student B: You care about the environment, as long as you don't have to do anything special or spend more money. You usually choose cost and convenience over health or concerns about the planet especially on expensive items like a washing machine or a fridge.

After some discussion, agree on a final list of at least five items of furniture and a range of cleaning products and groceries.

ACTIVITY

> **Brainstorming:**
> Make a list of three "natural" products that you already know of, or three common products that could be made naturally.
>
> *Examples:*
> *Herbal shampoo, solar-powered water heaters, battery powered cars*

Pick a product and create an advertisement for it. Your target market is your class. Consider the product's benefits to the consumer and the environment, the image that consumers will want to be associated with, and of course the price. Decide on an effective advertising campaign.

SPEECHES - Staying healthy

We can all do things to stay healthy. Think about what you do.

You are giving a talk to university students. Many students are stressed about exams, money, and the future. Some of them can't sleep because they're so worried; they can't focus during the day because they're too tired and many of them don't eat well.

> **Brainstorming:**
> What do you do to stay fit and healthy?
> What are some unhealthy activities you try to avoid?
> What do you do to relax and have fun?
> What could you do better?

Give the students some advice on how to relax and develop a healthier lifestyle. Consider these things:

- types of exercise to help with relaxation
- drinking less tea and coffee, but more water
- ways of getting more sleep
- making more effort to prepare or buy healthier food

Take notes. Organize your ideas. Present your speech to your classmates.

CONSOLIDATION AND RECYCLING

BUILDING VOCABULARY:

Circle the word that does not fit in each group.

1.	conservationist	ecologist	environmental	naturalist
2.	toxic	vigorous	lethal	poisonous
3.	natural	organic	treated	unaltered
4.	contaminate	filter	purify	clean
5.	in shape	healthy	ailing	on top form
6.	consumer	sustainable	customer	buyer
7.	nutrition	vitamins	minerals	illness
8.	product	disinfectant	plant	cleanser
9.	pesticides	modify	change	refine
10.	natural	organic	processed	whole

Work with a partner. Make sentences with one word from each group. Share them with another pair.

WRITING

Think of a restaurant you know. Write a review for it from the point of view of someone who is concerned with their health and the environment. Include the following topics in your review:

1. Food:
   • Are the ingredients organic?
   • Are the ingredients fresh and locally bought?
   • Is the food tasty?
   • How is it prepared?
   • How is it presented?

2. Environment:
   • Is the air clean?
   • Is smoking allowed in the restaurant?
   • Are there plants around?
   • Are the floors, tables, and dishes clean?

3. Overall impressions of the restaurant, the service and the experience.

Form groups. Take turns reading your reviews. Decide at which restaurant you would rather eat.

REFLECTION
1. How "natural" is your lifestyle already?
2. How would you change your lifestyle?
3. Do you think this will be more or less important as you get older? Why?

UNIT 9

Extreme Sports

Inga Vernon talks to her long-time friend and three-time BMX (Bicycle Motocross) champion Kurt Stevens to learn more about extreme sports.

What exactly is an extreme sport?

It can be any modern sport that isn't normal, isn't mainstream. It's considered risky and very stimulating. It can also be an ordinary activity that is done in an extraordinary way.

Like BMX riders doing tricks and stunts on a bicycle?

Exactly. A bicycle is usually used to go just from point A to point B, but when you take it further, when you do handstands on it or jump large gaps and add a dangerous element, then it's extreme.

What about the Tour de France? It can be risky and dangerous, right?

That's true and what they do is amazing. I could never ride that far. But, it's also ordinary. I mean, they're riding a bicycle on a road. That's normal.

So, something that's not normal, like bungee jumping. Do you consider that an extreme sport?

Sort of. What's considered extreme changes over time. Bungee jumping used to be extreme because it was edgy. Only a few people did it at first and it was a big deal. But now people can do it pretty safely in lots of places.

Maybe, but I still think jumping from a high place is pretty intense. You can't tell me bungee jumping isn't dangerous.

Sure, but it takes more than that to be labeled extreme. Take snowboarding. For a long time it was only an extreme sport. Risk takers, mostly young guys did it. It wasn't mainstream. You didn't see families out snowboarding together. But, more and more people started doing it. It became more respected and now it's lost its 'extremeness.' It was even added to the 1998 Nagano Olympics, right?

So, you mean being in the Olympics makes it less extreme?

Not just that. Maybe a better way to define if a sport is extreme or not is its reputation.

What do you mean, "reputation"?

It's all about the attitude surrounding it. Is it exciting? Will it make my adrenaline pump? Is it dangerous? Is it different from what ordinary people do? Is it edgy? I mean even running can be extreme.

Running? How can running be extreme?

Running in ways and in places where people don't normally run. For example, instead of going through a gate, an extreme runner would go over it, maybe with a flip or a jump. Or instead of running on the sidewalk, he'd run on walls or even on top of buildings. It makes it a little more of a challenge to go down the street. It's cool.

Wow, I never considered running an extreme sport.

Well, normal running isn't, but it's that little something extra. There are really no limits to what can be extreme. It's about pushing yourself. Like this guy I know who attached ice skates to his windsurfer and totally flew across the ice. That was crazy extreme!

VOCABULARY

Here are some words that will be useful in this unit. How many do you know? Work with a partner to figure out the meaning of any words that you don't know.

adrenaline	reputation	normal
amazing	risky	intense
attitude	stimulating	limits
challenge	stunts	mainstream
dangerous	extreme	risk taker

What other words can you think of to describe extreme sports?

VOCABULARY ACTIVITIES

A. Work with a partner. Choose a word from the list. Your partner will make a sentence. Take turns. Use your own ideas or ideas from the reading.

> Examples: Student A: *mainstream*
> Student B: *BMX stunt riding isn't a mainstream sport.*
> Student A: *stimulating*
> Student B: *Extreme sports are stimulating.*

Quick Fact
Zorbing is rolling down a hill inside a giant plastic ball.

B. Read the paragraph. Fill in the blanks. Work with a partner. Compare your answers. More than one answer may be possible.

Murderball is the slang name for rugby played by people in wheelchairs. It certainly pushes the _____ of standard sports. Teams of people who are paralyzed or partially paralyzed in their arms and legs play _____ each other. Players score by carrying the ball across a line at the end of the pitch. Teams slam into each other and try to knock opposing players over in order to _____ them from scoring. It's pretty _____ and certainly gets the players' _____ flowing. It has a _____ for being both tough and stimulating. It is an example of what can happen with a sport taken to the _____.

GRAPHIC ORGANIZER

Complete the organizer. Add any extreme sports you can think of, the equipment used, and any words you know related to the sport, the equipment, or both. Then work with a partner and compare your ideas. Can you think of sports that could become "extreme?" How would you do them differently?

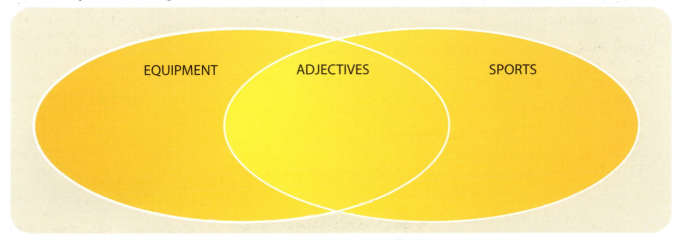

EQUIPMENT   ADJECTIVES   SPORTS

PRE-LISTENING QUESTIONS

1. Have you ever done an extreme sport?
2. Have you ever been injured?
3. Do you have friends who do things you think are dangerous?

SITUATION: *Lara doesn't want Jaycee to go to the skate park.*

Lara Hey, Jaycee, what are you doing this afternoon?

Jaycee I'm going to the new skate park. I can't wait to try it.

Lara You know I don't want you to go there. It's so dangerous. Remember when…

Jaycee There's nothing like it, Lara. You should try it some time. There's that adrenaline rush when you're in the air, that incredible feeling when you can finally do a stunt perfectly. I'd rather be skateboarding than just about anything else.

Lara Hold on, let me finish. What you're doing is so risky. You're just asking to get injured again.

Jaycee I'm not worried about it. If I thought about getting seriously hurt all the time, I'd never leave the house. You can get hurt doing just about anything.

Lara But your chances are greater…

Jaycee Greater than what?

Lara Wait a second. Could I please finish? Your chances are greater if you're doing crazy stunts on a skateboard. And what about other people? What happens if you get seriously injured? Do you…

Jaycee I'm not going to get hurt.

Lara Just listen, please! Do you really want to rely on other people to take care of you for the rest of your life?

Jaycee I think about it, but I can't allow myself to get worried about things like that. Part of doing an extreme sport is getting to know and testing your limits. When I first started skateboarding, I never would have tried any tricks. That would have been crazy. But now I know what I can and can't do. At least if I get hurt skateboarding, it'd be my own fault, not like in a car accident where I had no control.

Lara I give up. Just promise to give me a call when you get back from to the skate park, okay?

CHECK FOR UNDERSTANDING

1. What is Jaycee's extreme sport?
2. Why doesn't Lara like it?
3. Why does Jaycee feel confident he won't get hurt?
4. What do you think Lara and Jaycee's relationship is?

Work with a partner. Compare your answers.

Quick Fact
Inline skates were actually invented in the 18th century.

PRACTICE AND DISCUSSION

PERSONALIZATION

Complete these sentences with your own ideas.

> *There's nothing like...*
>
> *I'd rather be ... than just about anything else.*
>
> *If I worried about ... all the time, I'd never...*
>
> *People ... the time.*

Now share your sentences with a classmate.

DISCUSSION STRATEGIES - Asking not to be interrupted

Sometimes someone interrupts you, but you want to finish what you're saying. To let the person know to wait to talk, try the following expressions:

> Could I please finish?
> Hold that thought.
> Hold on (a second), let me finish.
> Wait, I'm almost done.
> Wait a second.
> Just listen/wait, please.

Quick Fact
The X Games first began in 1995 with summer games. Winter X Games began in 1998.

Discussion Strategy in Action

Listen to each conversation. What do the people say to keep from being interrupted?

1. _____
2. _____
3. _____

Discussion Practice

Work with a partner. Create a dialog for the following situation.

Student A: You really want to go ice climbing and you want Student B to go with you. Try to convince him or her. Student B might try to interrupt you, but don't let him or her.

Student B: You really don't want to go ice climbing and you don't want Student A to go either. Try to convince Student A to wait until it is warmer to go rock climbing then instead. Think of reasons why ice climbing in the mountains in winter is too dangerous. Interrupt to make your point.

Switch roles. This time Student A wants to go diving at the Great Barrier Reef.

FURTHER ACTIVITIES

ROLE PLAY

Work with a partner. Create a dialog for each of these situations.
Student A: You are a freestyle snowboarder.
Student B: You are Student A's best friend.

1. Student A has just won a gold medal at the X games.
   Student A, how would you react?
   Student B, what would you say to your friend?

2. Student A injured his/her back while doing a stunt in a
   competition and will be recovering in hospital and then
   at home for many months.
   Student B, what would you do or say to help him or her cope?
   Student A, how would you react?

Brainstorming:
What are some good and bad things that happen in extreme sports? How do people react when they are successful and how does that make other people, especially other competitors, feel?

How do you think a person would deal with being seriously hurt while doing an extreme sport? What could you do to help that person?

ACTIVITY

A television network is going to put together a show about less common extreme sports. They've come to you for help. They want to include five events. What events would you choose? You can use any "extreme" sport, including ones you and your classmates created earlier.

Work with a partner. Conduct a survey. Talk to your classmates and find out which sports they would like to see. Ideas to include in your survey:

1. What are they afraid of?
2. What are things they would do?
3. What are things they would never do?
4. What are things they would watch?
5. What are things they would never watch?

Now use your survey results to decide which events to include. Fill in the chart.

Events	Description
1. _____	_____
2. _____	_____
3. _____	_____
4. _____	_____
5. _____	_____

Finally, work in groups. Present your choices. Compare ideas and decide on the five events to include.

SPEECHES - My own extreme sport

What makes a sport extreme? Write your ideas down. Now follow these steps:

1. Think of something, a sport, a hobby, an activity, that is not extreme.
2. Look at your list of reasons a sport is extreme.
3. Figure out a way to make an ordinary activity into an extreme sport.
4. Present this new sport to the class. Explain the rules, what equipment is needed and
   what makes it extreme.

CONSOLIDATION AND RECYCLING

BUILDING VOCABULARY

Fill in the chart with the missing words. Then write eight sentences. Use words from the chart.

NOUN	VERB	ADJECTIVE
		risky
challenge		
limits		
stimulant		stimulating
	amaze	

_____

_____

_____

_____

_____

_____

_____

_____

Share your sentences with a classmate.

WRITING

Describe an activity. Imagine you are a student living away from home. You have decided to try an extreme sport. Write two emails:

> One email is to your friend. Tell your friend what you are doing and how happy you are.

> The other is to your family. You don't think they would approve, so you explain what you are doing and try to convince them that it is a good idea.

Work with a partner. Exchange emails and tell each other your reactions.

Quick Fact
Extreme Ironing is an everyday activity taken to the extreme. People take ironing boards to a remote location and iron a few items of clothing. Locations include a forest; a canoe; while snowboarding; the middle of a street; even underwater.

REFLECTION

1. What is one extreme sport you would really like to do?
2. What is one extreme sport you would never do?
3. How has your opinion of extreme sports changed?

Free Education

The United Nations Educational Scientific and Cultural Organization (UNESCO) constitution, signed in 1945, set out the importance of education and expressed a belief "in full and equal opportunities for education for all." Why then, so many years later, are more than 100 million children of primary school age not going to school?

To try to address the problem, in 1990 UNESCO launched 'Education for all by the year 2015' which identified six key education goals. Goal two is to provide free and compulsory primary education for all. The goals also contribute to the eight Millennium Development Goals, including MDG 2 on universal primary education and MDG 3 on gender equality in education, by 2015.

The international community has recognized primary education as a right because it has such a positive impact on people's lives and on society. One UNESCO report states that it gives access to further learning opportunities, helps a child to learn how to learn, and how to relate to other children, and it provides children with the tools for learning, such as reading, writing, and manipulating numbers. School also introduces children to the wider world.

However, while enrollment has been increasing, many children drop out before finishing the fifth grade. In Africa, for example, just 51 percent of children complete primary school. Low levels of enrollment and completion are concentrated in certain regions and also certain segments of the population. Poor children are less likely to attend school as are children in rural areas, children from ethnic and linguistic minorities, children with disabilities, and those affected by armed conflict.

Just being in school though is not enough and test results in some countries indicate that many students are learning virtually nothing. The motivation to learn only comes when education is seen to be worthwhile – and this depends on its quality. It is no good putting every child in school unless the education really enables them to learn and to go on learning and to acquire knowledge and skills that they can apply to their daily lives.

UNESCO goals do address quality issues, but some people believe there may be too much emphasis on providing free education rather than quality education. They argue that in some countries, people don't really value education if it's free and suggest that making a small, but affordable charge actually increases enrollment and quality.

The challenges of increasing access and improving quality reinforce each other because if schools cannot offer a quality education, parents are far less likely to send their children to school whether it is free or not.

Private schools, more often associated only with the rich, elite classes, could play an important part in providing good primary education even for poor children in low income countries.

VOCABULARY

Here are some words that will be useful in this unit. How many do you know? Work with a partner to figure out the meaning of any words that you don't know.

access	impact	goals
benefit	funding	sponsorship
compulsory	literacy	subsidize
elite	responsibility	tuition
fees	worthwhile	vocational

What other words and phrases do you know related to the topic?

VOCABULARY ACTIVITIES

A. Work with a partner. Take turns giving your opinions about the points raised in the reading. Use the vocabulary words.

Example: I think some governments will find it too expensive to provide free education to everyone. Perhaps some people's tuition could be subsidized by big international companies.

B. Fill in the blanks.

1. If you can read and write well, you are considered to have a good level of _____ .

2. In some countries, school is _____. Children must attend school until a certain age.

3. _____ training courses provide practical training for a specific occupation.

4. Education will not be universal until all children have _____ to it.

5. A good education system has a big _____ on the well-being of society.

GRAPHIC ORGANIZER

In groups or pairs, brainstorm what is the minimum level of education that a government should pay for and who should receive it. Discuss what areas of education to prioritize. Discuss where money should come from to pay for education.

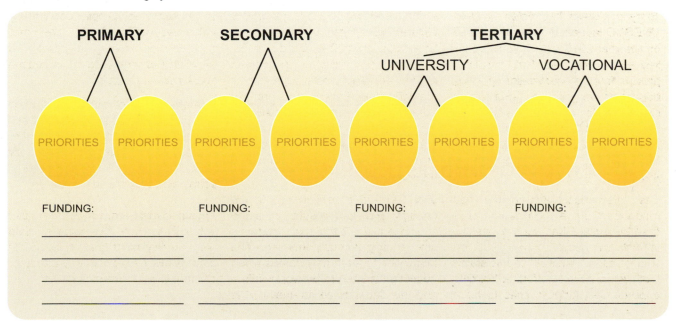

PRIMARY   SECONDARY   TERTIARY

UNIVERSITY   VOCATIONAL

PRIORITIES   PRIORITIES   PRIORITIES   PRIORITIES   PRIORITIES   PRIORITIES   PRIORITIES   PRIORITIES

FUNDING: FUNDING: FUNDING: FUNDING:

PRE-LISTENING QUESTIONS

1. Who is responsible for an individual's education?
2. Why might it be difficult for governments to provide free education?
3. What are other possible funding sources for schools besides the government?
4. Are there disadvantages of having funding from private sources such as large corporations?

SITUATION: *What are the strings?*

May   I can't believe that a pharmaceutical company is going to fund our new science lab.

Danny   Oh really, they are? That's really great news; we need a new lab.

May   I'm surprised to hear you say that. I think that it's terrible news.

Danny   Why's that? What's important is that we have a good, modern lab with facilities such as IT. The current one is a dinosaur.

May   That may be true, but do you want to look at a company logo every time you walk into the lab?

Danny   Frankly, I don't care. What I want to see is a well equipped lab, whatever the logo.

May   Give me a break. The fact of the matter is that 'gifts' like these don't come without strings attached. We know why soda companies sponsor school teams. They do it on the condition that they have the exclusive right to put vending machines in the schools. It increases their sales even though soda doesn't exactly lend itself to healthy living.

Danny   You have a point. But big corporations are not all bad. Some software companies are working with libraries to provide technology and training.

May   Don't get me wrong. I'm not saying they're all bad. But you have to wonder why a company would give all that money for a lab if there wasn't some payback for them. I wouldn't be surprised if a lot of the research we carry out will now be for their benefit. What if we found out things they didn't agree with – would they be published?

Danny   Don't be so paranoid. They would have to allow us to be independent.

May   I hate to say this but I think you're being naïve.

Danny   Well, I might be naïve but at least I'll be working in a state of the art lab.

> **Quick Fact**
> In 1496, it became compulsory for the eldest sons of certain wealthier groups of the population in Scotland to study Latin, the Arts, and law.

✓ CHECK FOR UNDERSTANDING

1. What is May upset about?
2. What does May mean by "gifts like these don't come without strings attached?"
3. What are Danny's main reasons to support the funding for the lab?
4. Why is May worried they won't be allowed to be independent?
5. Who do you agree with more, May or Danny?

Work with a partner. Compare your answers.

PERSONALIZATION

Complete these sentences with your own ideas.

I can't believe that…
I heard that…
I hate to have to say this but…
What I want to see…
I hope that…
What's important is…

Now share your sentences with a classmate.

DISCUSSION STRATEGIES - Conceding but disagreeing

In a discussion, it's important to acknowledge when the other person has a valid point, even if you don't agree with it. This is called conceding. Often we concede reluctantly with phrases such as *I'm afraid you're right*. After conceding the other person's point, you can then show you disagree by presenting more information using *but* or *however*.

You have a point, but…
I'm afraid you're right; however…
I hate to say it, but…
I might be being naïve but…

You may be right but…
Don't get me wrong…
That may be true, but…

Discussion Strategy in Action

Listen to the conversations. Which phrases from the discussion strategy do the speakers use? What is the situation?

	Phrase	Situation
1.	_____	_____
2.	_____	_____
3.	_____	_____
4.	_____	_____

Discussion Practice

Work with a partner. Create a dialog for the following situations using the discussion strategy of conceding but disagreeing:

1. Your friend tells you about a fantastic university but you think it's too far away from your family and you will have to borrow too much money to go there.

2. Your cousin wants to go into vocational training to become an electrician, but he is so good at mathematics that you think he should go to university.

3. You want to volunteer to teach in a poor primary school in Africa for a couple of years, but your father thinks that you will be wasting your education and you should concentrate on getting a good job in your own country.

FURTHER ACTIVITIES

ROLE PLAY

In a debate each speaker presents a different point of view on a particular topic. A formal debate follows a set of rules and procedures. An informal debate can be a casual discussion between friends or colleagues.

> **Brainstorming:**
>
> What kinds of formal debates have you listened to or been involved with? How did they develop?
>
> Do you ever debate ideas with your friends? How can you tell if someone has won a debate?

Work with a partner. Have an informal debate on the following topics. Remember to think about ideas, both for and against the topic, before you begin.

1. Everyone should have access to university education.
2. There should be an international fund to pay for primary education in countries that can't afford it.

ACTIVITY

Work in small groups. Imagine that you have $10 million to spend on school improvements at a local school. Create a proposal for what you would do. Consider these aspects:

- Would you make changes in buildings, programs, fees or other things?
- What kind of changes would have the most impact and who would benefit most from them?
- Could any of the changes be made sustainable and self-funding in the long term?

Present your plan to the class. The class will vote on the best one.

SPEECHES - Presentation

> There is an engineering school that has always been very popular. The entrance exam is very difficult and it takes many years of intense study to prepare for it. Less than 10% of the students who apply, actually pass the exam. A degree from the school is very prestigious and usually leads to an excellent, well paid job.
>
> The school is considering making the entrance exam easier. It also aims to let in more women. Both ideas should allow more students to have access to the educational opportunities there. The funding for the increased number of students will partly come from a new corporate sponsor.

Work in groups of four. Choose one of the roles and prepare a short presentation.
Then present it to your classmates.

Student applicant: You are in favor of making the entrance exam easier. You think that as many students as possible should have access to the school. You think that it's a shame that there are so few female students.

Graduate from the school: You are against this change because you worked very hard for your degree and increased student numbers might devalue it. You don't think that women should get special treatment.

President/Dean of the engineering school: You are worried that expansion will increase pressure on your resources. You might need more funding from private sources and you don't want to lose your independence.

Corporate sponsor: You see this as an excellent opportunity to develop your reputation, prepare future employees, and carry out useful research at the school. You are also interested in hiring more female engineers so that you can be seen as an equal opportunity employer.

CONSOLIDATION AND RECYCLING

BUILDING VOCABULARY

Fill in the blanks using vocabulary from this unit.

Even at universities which are heavily 1._____ by the government, finding money for tuition 2._____ and living costs is always an issue for students and their families. Some countries like Australia and Singapore offer their students bonded 3._____. Although these are very generous, students are required to work for a public hospital, organization, or company for a period of time. This is usually a similar number of years as the students take to complete their 4._____.

The advantage of this system is that students 5._____ from a good education and do not have the burden of a 6._____ to repay at the end of their studies. While giving all students 7._____ to university it also makes them take 8._____ for their own education. The government also benefits because the educated population works for it and stays in the country longer. However, many 9._____ find this frustrating. They have to work for lower wages and are not free to pursue potentially lucrative 10._____ immediately.

Work with a partner. According to the article, what are the advantages and disadvantages of bonded scholarships?

WRITING

Your school wants to expand its library and is considering allowing corporate sponsorship. A large publishing company is prepared to sponsor the library. The company has several conditions:

The professors will have to choose a certain percentage of the publisher's books and electronic materials for their courses and the students will be required to buy them.

The publishing company will also have first refusal on publishing any new research that comes out of the university.

How do you feel about this? Write a letter to the school. Give your reasons for or against the proposal. Exchange letters with a classmate. Write a response. Compare your letters.

REFLECTION

1. How can we have truly free education?
2. What are the hard decisions individuals, institutions, and governments have to make about education?
3. Is there really one ideal system?

UNIT 11
Multiple Intelligences

Are athletes more intelligent than some scientists? Why do some people find learning languages easy, but struggle with mathematics? Why do others excel at sports but can't play a musical instrument? The theory of Multiple Intelligences (M I) tries to provide answers to questions like these.

Instead of thinking of intelligence as the ability to score high marks on an academic test, M I theory defines several types of intelligence, each one an equally important strength. Everyone has each of the eight or more intelligences, but some intelligences are more dominant than others. Where do your strengths lie?

INTELLIGENCE	DEFINITION	QUALITIES
Verbal-Linguistic (Word Smart)	The ability to communicate well with words.	You have good listening skills and are often very articulate and an effective speaker.
Mathematical-Logical (Number or Reasoning Smart)	The ability to reason and work well with numbers.	You can easily make connections between pieces of information. You are often skilled at experimenting, problem solving and categorizing information.
Musical (Music Smart)	The ability to produce and appreciate music and sounds.	You think in sounds, rhythms, and patterns. You have an immediate reaction to music, often easily recognizing and remembering melodies.
Visual-Spatial (Picture Smart)	The ability to create mental images. You are artistic.	You think in pictures. Your skills can include drawing, painting, understanding charts, and having a good sense of direction.
Bodily-Kinesthetic (Body Smart)	The ability to control body movements well and be skilled at handling objects.	You are often good at sports. You communicate and remember information through movement and learn by physically carrying out ideas. You learn by doing.
Interpersonal (People or Social Smart)	The ability to work well with others and be sensitive to other people's feelings, intentions, and motivations.	Your skills include communicating (verbally and non-verbally), building trust and co-operating with others.
Intrapersonal (Self Smart)	The ability to assess and understand your own behavior, strengths, and limitations.	Your skills include reflecting on and analyzing desires and dreams and evaluating how you interact with others. You know who you are.
Naturalist (Nature Smart)	The ability to understand the natural world, to identify and classify plants, animals, and other natural elements.	You are usually very aware of the environment.

The theory has had an impact on teaching methods. Traditionally, teachers have focused on just two of the intelligences - mathematical and verbal skills. Think of some of the greatest athletes and actors, where would they be today if they had only relied on their verbal-linguistic and mathematical intelligence? As a result of this theory, a growing trend in education is to incorporate many different ways to teach and to test.

VOCABULARY

Here are some words that will be useful in this unit. How many do you know? Work with a partner to figure out the meaning of any words that you don't know.

analytical	**evaluate**	**movement**
articulate	**excel**	**motivation**
assess	**identify**	**patterns**
classify	**incorporate**	**strengths**
dominant	**logical**	**technical**

What other words and phrases do you know related to the topic?

VOCABULARY ACTIVITIES

A. Work with a partner. Use at least two of the words above and one of the phrases below to describe one of the intelligences in your own words. Your partner must guess which one it is.

communication skills	**growing trend**	**be sensitive to**	**physical activities**
hand-eye coordination	**reflect on**	**build trust**	**excel at**
create a mental image	**interact with**	**carry out**	**care about**

B. Work with a partner. Describe someone you both know who is strong in one of the intelligences. Use the words and phrases above. Your partner will guess who and which intelligence you are describing. Take turns.

GRAPHIC ORGANIZER

Fill in the chart. Use the reading and your own ideas. Add at least one more job and one person for each type of intelligence. The people can be someone you know or someone famous. Then work with a partner and compare your ideas. Give reasons for the people you chose. Why is it possible for them to be in more than one category?

TYPES OF INTELLIGENCE	STRENGTHS	POSSIBLE JOBS	EXAMPLES
WORD SMART		*journalist,*	
NUMBER OR REASONING SMART		*computer programmer,*	
MUSIC SMART		*musician,*	
PICTURE SMART		*photographer,*	
BODY SMART		*dancer,*	
PEOPLE OR SOCIAL SMART		*salesperson,*	
SELF SMART		*religious leader,*	
NATURE SMART		*gardener,*	

PRE-LISTENING QUESTIONS

1. Do you agree with the theory of multiple intelligences?
2. Do you know anyone who is a very good musician or artist, but doesn't do well in school?
3. Do you feel that the teachers value verbal and mathematical intelligences more than other intelligences?

SITUATION: *Jacob can't see why art is being used to teach math.*

Jacob I'm struggling with my art class. Even though I'm a math major I'm required to take an art class. It feels like a huge waste of time.

Amy Give it a chance. We've studied about multiple intelligences in my teacher training classes. Everyone has a range of intelligences but it's clear that people have different strengths though. Take you and me. You like numbers and solving problems. I'm good at writing and explaining things. So let's just say that we're both very smart, but you score higher than me in math but a little lower in your artistic intelligence.

Jacob Whatever. It can't mean that everyone is equally intelligent though, can it? Logically, that's all wrong. It doesn't make sense to me.

Amy No, it doesn't mean people are equally intelligent. It means we're intelligent in different ways. We have different strengths and the important thing is we learn in different ways. If a teacher uses a variety of activities, more students will learn. For example, a teacher can do more than just write numbers on the board; he or she could also use pictures, and music, and poetry to teach mathematics.

Jacob Yeah, but a written test is the only way to really measure intelligence.

Amy Think about it. Traditional written tests only focus on verbal and math skills. Suppose someone doesn't do well on a written test? It might just mean that that test isn't a good way to measure that person's intelligences. Maybe having that person draw a picture or write a song would be better.

Jacob So, how do you compare intelligences, say for university entrance? Where do you stop with the intelligences? I hear that there may even be a football intelligence.

Amy I hadn't heard about football intelligence, but it's true other classifications are being proposed. But I think you're missing my point. Basically, what I'm saying is it will help a lot of people if we all start looking at intelligence differently. It will change our schools and yes, sometimes you may have to do things that you're not so good at, but ultimately, more students will feel successful and they'll be more motivated to learn.

Jacob Okay, you win. Anyway I can't get out of my art class so I may as well make the best of it. Maybe I'll discover my own inner artistic intelligence.

Amy Maybe. Who knows?

CHECK FOR UNDERSTANDING

1. Why is Jacob upset?
2. What strengths do Jacob and Amy each have?
3. What are Jacob's and Amy's views about multiple intelligences?
4. Who do you agree with more, Jacob or Amy?

Work with a partner. Compare your answers.

Quick Fact
The years before children go to school could be the most important years for learning. Many of the connections in the brain are made in first six years of life.

PRACTICE AND DISCUSSION

PERSONALIZATION

Complete these sentences with your own ideas.

> *I am struggling with…*
> *I am good at…*
> *…makes sense to me*
> *I can't get out of…*
> *I may as well make the best of ….*

Now share your sentences with a classmate.

DISCUSSION STRATEGIES - Strongly disagreeing

Sometimes in a conversation we don't agree with someone and want to dispute what they say. Depending on the relationship and the situation, this can be very direct ("That's not true.") or a little more diplomatic ("I see it differently."). Below are ways to strongly disagree with another person's idea.

That's not true.	I think you have it wrong.
(I think), You're wrong about…	I think there's another way to look at it.
(I'm sure) You're mistaken.	I see it differently.
That just isn't so.	

Discussion Strategy in Action

Listen to the conversations. What is the main topic? What is the relationship between the speakers?

	Main topic	Relationship
1.	_____	_____
2.	_____	_____
3.	_____	_____

Work with a partner. Take turns making statements and disagreeing.

Discussion Practice

Work with a partner. Create a short dialog using the discussion strategies for each of the following situations.

1. Your friend is very upset because she isn't doing well in school. She is a fantastic dancer and an excellent artist. Try to convince her that she is intelligent, but in ways that aren't measured in most of her exams.

2. The teacher gave you an assignment to write about an important event in your life. You aren't good at writing and want to write a song instead. Your teacher doesn't think a song will work.

3. Your friend doesn't like to read manuals. He finds he learns best by doing something, not just reading about it. Give your friend some suggestions about ways to learn more about how to use his new camera.

FURTHER ACTIVITIES

ROLE PLAY

A strong team is one in which people work together effectively. One way to have a stronger team is to bring together people with different dominant strengths or intelligences. Work in groups of four. Choose one of the following situations. Present your solution to the class.

1. The local sports club is holding a 'mini-olympics' for children in order to raise money. A number of people have offered to help. May is body smart; Ali is word smart; Ken is people smart, and Lee is art smart. Use your understanding of multiple intelligences to decide what each person should do.

2. Four climbers are stuck on a mountain expedition with no phone. Tony has sprained his ankle. Tina is picture smart, Mark is body smart, and Eric is nature smart. Decide what each person should do to help Tony.

3. A building developer has applied for permission to cut down a small forest in order to build a plastics factory. Some people living near the forest want to take action to stop the development: Ling is music smart, Rick is body smart, Terry is nature smart, and Suzy is people smart. Decide how they can work together and what each of them can do.

ACTIVITY

Read the quiz on page 96 and label each box with the correct intelligence.

Word smart	Number smart	Body smart
People smart	Music smart	Picture smart
Self smart	Nature smart	

Then answer the quiz questions to find out what your dominant intelligences are. Read each statement. Write the number that best represents your response next to each statement. The categories with the higher totals represent your stronger intelligences.

Compare your results with a partner or in a small group.

SPEECHES - You are the teacher

Your school has decided to apply the Multiple Intelligence Theory in the classroom. Look at the topics below. Decide ways you would teach the information so students who have different dominant intelligences will understand it. Use art, music, song, stories, movement, charts, student writing, and any other activities you can think of. Present your ideas in groups.

1. For young children: learning to add the numbers 1-10.
2. For older students: an important event in your country's history.

CONSOLIDATION AND RECYCLING

BUILDING VOCABULARY

What's your opinion? Mark your answers. Then discuss them with your classmates.

IDEA	TRUE	FALSE
The theory of multiple intelligences gives us more and better ways of classifying intelligence.		
People who can create mental images easily are never very good at logic.		
Usually, men are better at analyzing and women are better at communicating.		
People who are good at math often recognize patterns easily.		
It is impossible for teachers to teach and evaluate more than two or three different types of intelligence.		

Work with a partner. Make a sentence about someone's intelligences. Your partner will guess which of the intelligences you are referring to. Take turns.

Example:
A: My friend is a great singer. She plays the piano and the flute, too.
B: So, she's got strong musical intelligence.
A: Yes, she has.

WRITING

Write a letter to the local newspaper. Choose one of the following topics:

- why the multiple intelligences theory should or should not be implemented in primary or secondary schools
- why written intelligence tests should or should not be the only test used to measure a student's intelligence

Work with a partner. Exchange letters. Compare your ideas.

REFLECTION
1. What is intelligence?
2. How do you identify intelligence in yourself and others?
3. How have your views about who should be considered "intelligent" changed from the beginning of the unit?

UNIT 12

Gender Roles

There was a time, not that long ago, when all men went out to work and women stayed at home to take care of the house and children. The accompanying stereotypes were fairly rigid: men were strong and unemotional while women were weak and submissive. Now, when you walk down the street you might see a fashionably dressed man with highlights in his hair or a woman in overalls directing a building site. From career choices to clothing styles, the distinction between what is considered masculine and feminine is becoming more ambiguous, perhaps even androgynous, and gender roles are less defined.

The breakdown of gender barriers obviously opens up more opportunities for women in terms of jobs, relationships, lifestyle, and personal development, but what does it do for men? On a consumer level there is little doubt that the personal care industry is booming, there are now whole floors of department stores devoted to men's cosmetics and fashion. On an emotional level, men seem to be embracing a more sensitive, communicative, and flexible approach to life and relationships.

Will these gradually evolving changes continue, or are there still fundamental behavioral differences between men and women?

Some research seems to indicate that men's and women's brains may behave differently: women's brains seem to have developed to be more attuned to empathizing,

understanding another person's feelings and thoughts, whereas men's brains are geared more for understanding systems and how things work, and finding solutions. This means that a woman and a man can interpret an identical situation in very different ways.

Differences in communication, learning, and behavior can be seen from an early age. Girls and boys tend to relate very differently, especially when put in single sex groups. Girls generally try to create connections with individuals, a close friend or two, whereas boys tend to be more focused on activities - often within a large group and with various layers of status. The boys often concentrate on demonstrating skills, challenging others, and resisting challenges.

Gender roles and behavioral differences continue into the workplace. In the recent past, people would sometimes react very badly to a woman entering what had formerly been a male-only workplace or vice versa. The problems were more serious when the newcomer started at a senior level and introduced changes to the way the people worked. While some jobs are still dominated by either men or women, they are the exceptions now, and even in these jobs there are fewer workplace conflicts.

Gender differences may be linked to our physical differences and the way our brains are formed, but more important are the outside factors, notably the reactions of others, especially our peers and role models.

VOCABULARY

Here are some words that will be useful in this unit. How many do you know? Work with a partner to figure out the meaning of any words that you don't know.

ambiguous	breakdown	find solutions
androgynous	communication style	masculine
behavior	empathize	misunderstanding
biological	feminine	stereotype

What other words and phrases do you know related to the topic?

VOCABULARY ACTIVITIES

A. Match the word to the definition.

✓1. stereotype   _d_   a. to accept without resistance
✓2. empathize   _j_   b. relating to male or female sex
✓3. passive   _a_   c. to have parts in common
✓4. gender   _b_   d. often oversimplified description of individual or group
✓5. masculine   _e_   e. relating to men or boys
✓6. feminine   _i_   f. the way people act
✓7. ambiguous   _h_   g. having characteristics that are both male and female
✓8. androgynous   _g_   h. having more than one possible meaning
✓9. intersect   _c_   i. relating to women or girls
✓10. behavior   _f_   j. to understand and feel for another's situation or feelings

B. Work with a partner. Take turns making new sentences with the words above.

GRAPHIC ORGANIZER

Think about the ideas expressed in the reading passage about males and females. List the similarities and differences in the appropriate part of the diagram. Then work with a partner and compare your ideas.

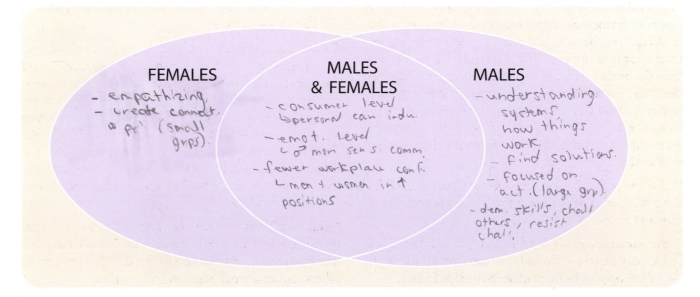

FEMALES
- empathizing,
- create connect.
- pref (small grps).

MALES & FEMALES
- consumer level
  └ personal can indu.
- emot. level
  └ ♂ more sens. comm.
- fewer workplace conf.
  └ men + women in ↑ positions

MALES
- understanding systems, how things work
- find solutions.
- focused on act. (large grp).
- dem. skills, chall others, resist chall.

PRE-LISTENING QUESTIONS

1. How are men and women different? Say at least three ways.
2. Do you think that certain jobs are more suitable for women or men?

SITUATION: *Emily wants to be an engineer.*

Emily Guess what? I finally decided to major in engineering. It was a hard decision especially because my parents wanted me to become a nurse or a teacher. Even my advisor tried to talk me out of it. I couldn't believe it! Why can't women be engineers? What century is this?

Tom Your parents and advisor have a point. You should choose a major that suits your strengths.

Emily Right, and that's just why I went for engineering.

Tom The fact is that men and women are not the same genetically, physically, emotionally or otherwise. If I were in a burning building, I wouldn't want a woman to come rescue me. Would you? I don't think she could carry me down the stairs.

Emily And what does that have to do with my deciding to be an engineer? I don't plan to carry people. Anyway, you can't stereotype that way, there are plenty of women working as firefighters nowadays. But both men and women should be encouraged to choose any career they want. This is nothing new. I've been reading about the ancient Egyptians. For thousands of years, women could enter into contracts, own property, and get the same pay for the same work as men.

Tom Let's face it, that's one of the few exceptions. Anyway, how do you explain the low numbers of women in computers, math, and science. And, what about the high numbers of women in education and journalism now? Women have choices, but you still don't see a lot of female computer geeks. How do you account for that?

Emily I think if more girls were given more support, they would go into computing, math, and science if they wanted to. This is starting to happen, but changes take time. Look at the number of female engineers now. There are more than, say, twenty years ago.

Tom Maybe, but I still have to disagree with you. The fact is, there aren't a lot of female engineers and I think it's because women aren't good at it.

Emily Well, I am. So, I'm not going to worry about it.

CHECK FOR UNDERSTANDING

What are the main points Tom and Emily make?

TOM	EMILY
_____	_____
_____	_____
_____	_____
_____	_____

Work with a partner. Compare your answers.

Quick Fact
Women represent just over 40 per cent of the global workforce.

PRACTICE AND DISCUSSION

PERSONALIZATION

Complete these sentences with your own ideas.

> *If I were ... I wouldn't ...*
> *The fact is that men and women ...*
> *I don't think ...*
> *How do you explain ...*
> *I think if ...*

Now share your sentences with a classmate.

Quick Fact
In 2006, just 9% of the senior judiciary, 10% of senior police officers, and 13% of editors of national newspapers in the UK were women.

DISCUSSION STRATEGIES - Support your opinions

When you're having a discussion, it's often useful to support your statement or point of view with examples and facts that you know. This clarifies what you mean and gives more strength to your point of view.

Look at the…
Think about the…
What about the…
How do you explain the…

The fact is…
I know for a fact…
Have you noticed…
You can't deny that…

Discussion Strategy in Action

Listen to the conversations. What examples or facts do the speakers use to support their statements?

1. _____

2. _____

3. _____

4. _____

Work with a partner. Take turns making statements supported with facts or reasons.

Discussion Practice

Work with a partner. You don't agree on the following points. Discuss them using facts or examples to support your arguments.

Brainstorming:
What types of statements would you make?
How would you support them?
How would you agree/disagree?

1. You think that most men do/don't do their fair share of the housework.
2. You think that men and women are/aren't better at different kinds of jobs.
3. You think that life was easier/harder for men/women in the past.

FURTHER ACTIVITIES

ROLE PLAY

Work with a partner. Create a dialog for each of the following situations. Support your choices and convince your partner that your idea is better.

1. A girl is shopping with her friend. He has chosen clothes that she doesn't think are appropriate; for example, because of the color. He points out some facts about current fashion to support his shopping choices.

2. It is Saturday night. It has been a long, busy week and you want to go out and have some fun. You have very different ideas on what would be a fun night out. Discuss what you want to do.

ACTIVITY

Work in small groups. Think of at least three ways men's and women's lives have changed in the last twenty years. Compare your ideas with the rest of the class and make a list of all the ideas. Discuss what still needs to change in order to have more equal relationships between men and women.

SPEECHES - Interview (unfair treatment) – didn't do

Work with a partner.

Student A: You are a student doing research about gender equality. Part of your research is to interview men and women about their experiences. Ask the following questions and some more questions of your own:

- Do you think some people have or have not been hired just because of their gender?
- Do you think that there are fewer opportunities at school or in the workplace because of gender?
- Are there times when it's a clear advantage to be a man/woman? Give examples.
- Do you remember situations in which you felt gender was an issue? Give examples.
- Were you ever discouraged from doing something because of your gender?
- What would you say are the most common gender stereotypes?

Student B: You are being interviewed. Think about experiences (real or imaginary) you have had. Answer the questions. Give facts and examples.

After the interview, work with another pair. Report and discuss the answers to the interview questions.

CONSOLIDATION AND RECYCLING

BUILDING VOCABULARY:

Work with a partner. Look at the words and phrases in the chart (you may need to look up some of them in a dictionary). Discuss if you have seen them used more often to describe men, or women, or both. Some of them can be negative – do you know which ones?

petite		small	
absent-minded		distracted	
witty		entertaining	
beautiful		handsome	
forceful		strident	
assertive		reserved	
a real dude		a real babe	
chick		guy	
fiery		volatile	
emotional		expressive	
timid		tough	

Make a list of other words from this unit and other units that are usually used to describe either males or females. Which words are linked to or promote gender stereotypes? Why could this be a problem?

WRITING

Work with a partner. Write a description of one famous male and one famous female celebrity.

Include the following:
- a description of his/her physical characteristics
- a description of his/her personality
- some information about what he/she has done
- any other information you think is important

Read your descriptions aloud without mentioning the name of the person. See if your classmates can guess who you are describing.

Quick Fact
In China, around 117 boys are born for every 100 girls. The global ratio is around 105 boys for every 100 girls.

REFLECTION

1. What is gender?
2. How have your views about male and female roles changed from the beginning of the unit?
3. Will roles continue to change?

Dating

Speed dating is becoming more popular in large cities in China. Zhu Yi talks to some speed daters to see why.

In one night, each male spends just seven minutes with each female, each of them trying to impress their new partner, ask questions and decide if they have chemistry before moving on. When the evening ends, they list who they hit it off with and want to meet again.

Jinyi, a 22-year-old university student, believes this is a more effective way to date. "I'm tired of people trying to set me up, especially on blind dates. It was hard enough not meeting the person beforehand, but then finding out that we didn't have anything in common was such a waste of time. I like to dance and go to movies. Most of the women my family and friends set me up with didn't like these things. I didn't see how I would ever get along with any of them. The old saying that opposites attract doesn't seem to hold true for me."

Many young people are attracted to casual dating. They don't like to be bound by the responsibilities of a serious relationship. Jinyi turned to speed dating because he wants more. "At least I know that everyone here is looking for a potential partner," he said, adding that turning someone down is pretty painless too.

Some of the other modern dating options such as personal ads and online dating concern Jinyi and his friends. Luli, a 21-year-old student from Wuhan explained, "While you can remain anonymous searching through many profiles online, you are never sure the person is who they say they are. I mean the online 'man of my dreams' could actually be a murderer for all I know."

Luli admits that for her, first impressions are very important, "I take into account a person's appearance and our initial chemistry when deciding whether I want to see that person again. Speed dating attracts me because I get that first impression and I don't have to spend a lot of time sifting through numerous profiles and waiting for emails that may never come."

Jinyi and Luli both said they feel able to ask more personal questions and don't have to work up the courage to ask someone out, or worry about pick-up lines that fail. If nothing happens romantically they may at least develop friendships and who knows who they will meet through these friendships.

VOCABULARY

Here are some words that will be useful in this unit. How many do you know? Work with a partner to figure out the meaning of any words that you don't know.

hit it off	to set someone up	move on
get along with	to ask someone out	have chemistry
go on a blind date	turn someone down	first impressions
opposites attract	pick someone up	partner
to see someone	have something in common	

What other words and phrases do you know related to the topic?

VOCABULARY ACTIVITIES

A. Fill in the blanks with phrases from the list above.

Juan: I met someone last night who was great! We really _____.
          They say first impressions are very important. When we first met, I knew we would like each other!

Jia: Last night was terrible! My friend set me up. I went on _____.
          We had nothing in common. I couldn't wait for the date to be over.

Kimi: Well, that guy at work finally _____ me _____ for Saturday night.
          I had to turn him down though. I have to work on Saturday.

B. Partner A: Say a sentence using a phrasal verb from the reading.
   Partner B: Make a new sentence, replacing the phrasal verb.

   Example:
   Student A: We didn't hit it off.
   Student B: We didn't like each other.

Quick Fact
Australia: Teens tend to go out in large groups and don't usually become couples until 18 or 19. Girls may ask boys out and pay for dates.

GRAPHIC ORGANIZER

Create a mind map on dating using the ideas in the reading and your own ideas. Then work with a partner and compare your ideas.

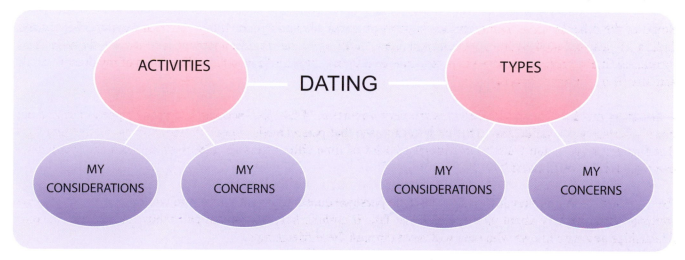

POINTS OF VIEW *Online dating is not real.*

PRE-LISTENING QUESTIONS

1. What are some advantages/disadvantages to online dating?
2. How is it like speed dating or other forms of dating?
3. Would you consider this method of dating? Why?

SITUATION: *Sam and David discuss the pros and cons of online dating.*

Sam	Online dating is the way to go. It's so much better than speed dating. You can spend time building a real emotional connection and get to know someone. Then decide if you want to meet in person. Plus, it's safe. You don't have to let them know your real name, location or telephone number. You have more control over what happens.
David	Yeah, but the person could be married, or involved with someone else, or even a criminal. How can you know for sure?
Sam	I see your point, but I'm not worried about that; I'm a pretty good judge of people. Going online is a good way to meet a lot of people. It's easy to search for those people I think I'll be compatible with and weed out those I don't click with - I just don't answer them.
David	It's not my idea of a good time. I mean you spend hours chatting online with people you may never meet and end up ignoring the real people around you. Meeting people through friends or activities is a much better way to go.
Sam	I understand what you're saying, but it's really not like that. I'm a lot more comfortable with online dating. I always felt so awkward trying to flirt with someone face to face. I feel like I've definitely improved my communication skills by dating online.
David	Maybe it's just me then. I'm not fond of spending a lot of time on the computer anyway. You can get so isolated. I know you think you are with other people when you are online, but for me, it's not the same as going out and being with people. Staying at the computer, you risk losing your chance for a real relationship.
Sam	I'm afraid we are going to have to agree to disagree. I mean, I guess it doesn't suit everyone, but it's certainly working for me. I don't get all embarrassed and stressed out like I used to on dates. Now, when I meet someone, we already know a lot about each other so we quickly get over the awkwardness of a traditional first date. I've become friends with more women in the few months since I started online dating than ever before, and I've been on some great dates!

CHECK FOR UNDERSTANDING

1. Why does Sam like online dating? List the reasons.
2. Why doesn't David like online dating? List the reasons.
3. What expressions do they use to agree and disagree?

Work with a partner. Compare your answers.

Quick Fact
Mobile phone dating services now also allow people to meet, chat, and possibly become romantically involved.

PERSONALIZATION

Complete these sentences with your own ideas.

I don't think it's possible to…
I'm not really fond of…
…is not my idea of a good time.
…is the way to go.
I hate to admit it, but…

Now share your sentences with a classmate.

DISCUSSION STRATEGIES - Saying no nicely

Listed below are a few ways that we can say no without hurting the other person's feelings.
Can you think of other ways that you may have heard?

Sorry, I'm busy.
Thank you, but I have to…
Thanks, but I have something scheduled.
I'm afraid I can't…

Sorry, I have other plans.
Thanks for asking, but…
Thanks, but I'm not (really) fond of…

Discussion Strategy in Action

Listen. For each conversation, answer these questions:
    A. What is the invitation for?
    B. Does the person accept or decline the invitation?

1. _____
2. _____
3. _____

Discussion Practice

Work with a partner. Create a dialog for the following situations.

1. You have two tickets to a concert. You want to ask your partner out. Decide what type of concert it is, when it is, and where. Your partner doesn't want to go because of the type of music it is.

2. You ask your partner to go dancing on Saturday night. Your partner has to work. You change it to Friday night. Your partner still can't go.

Quick Fact
Afghanistan: Almost all Schools for boys and girls are separate so dating is less common. Marriages are often arranged by parents.

FURTHER ACTIVITIES

ROLE PLAY

Form groups of at least four students for some speed dating. You will have three minutes with each partner. Your teacher will keep time. Practice saying no nicely and using other expressions you have learned in this unit.

> **Brainstorming:**
> What types of questions would you ask?
> How would you express interest/disinterest?

ACTIVITY

Are you best suited for conventional dating, online dating or speed dating?
Take the quiz on page 97 to find out.

SPEECHES - Talk show

Imagine you are on a talk show about dating. Form groups of at least five students. Choose one of the roles below to play on the talk show. How would their opinions differ?

Parents

Industry representatives from a dating agency

University students (male and female)

Psychologists

TV show host

Use the questions below to prepare for your role.
Think about how your character would answer them.
Also think about other questions you would ask the other people on the talk show.

- Should people date?
- How do/did you date?
- What type of person is the ideal date?
- What is the right age to start dating?
- What is acceptable behavior on a first date?
- Who pays for the first dates?
- Will online/speed dating become the standard form of dating?
- Is it okay to show affection in public?

Introduce yourselves on the talk show and then share your ideas about dating.

Dating

Are you best suited for conventional dating, online dating, or speed dating? Take the quiz to find out.

1. The best way to find a potential partner is:
   a. through friends/parents.
   b. through the Internet.
   c. through a dating service.

2. Which way do you feel most comfortable expressing yourself?
   a. In writing.
   b. Face to face.
   c. Over the phone.

3. When you meet someone, you are first attracted to:
   a. appearance.
   b. personality.
   c. both.

4. "Love at first sight."
   a. Does not exist.
   b. Happens everyday.
   c. Is possible.

5. Who should pay for a date?
   a. The person who asked.
   b. Each person should pay half.
   c. The man.

6. When you go on a date, are you looking to:
   a. casually date?
   b. date someone seriously?
   c. get married soon?

7. Your ideal date includes:
   a. going out with a group of people.
   b. meeting in a virtual café.
   c. going to dinner followed by a walk on the beach.

8. For a lasting relationship it's better if:
   a. you have little in common — it keeps the relationship exciting.
   b. you know nothing about each other beforehand.
   c. you have a lot in common — the more things you share the better.

9. Describe your availability to go on dates.
   a. I have a lot of time to date.
   b. I don't have any time to date.
   c. It's easier if it's part of my other activities.

10. Having your parents' approval of the person you date is:
    a. very important.
    b. important, but not all I consider.
    c. not something I care about too much.

	a	b	c		a	b	c
1.	1	3	5	6.	3	5	1
2.	3	5	1	7.	5	3	1
3.	5	3	1	8.	1	3	5
4.	3	5	1	9.	1	5	3
5.	3	5	1	10.	1	5	3

Look at your answers and add up your score. find the description that matches your score.

0 - 16 points You are a conventional date prefer to meet people through traditional, sources, such as parents and friends, a important that your parents like your partne enjoy creating romantic dates such as c dinners and walks on a beach. You have free time to meet people. You are lookin serious relationship, possibly marriage.

17 - 33 points You are an Internet da communicate best in writing. You focus building an emotional and intellectual c over appearance. You have a busy sche can make time to date if it's part of your You like the adventure and anonymity of world. You don't care what your parents just want to date casually, nothing seriou

34 - 50 points You are a speed dater. sight exists for you. You don't have very time so having as many dates as possi you greatest chance of having th moment'. You need all the help you c prefer to communicate with people fac you often judge them on appearance.

Does this quiz accurately describe why not?

Unit 13 Activity

> **Quick Fact**
> Europe: Young people often date in groups. In Spain, teens might join a pandilla, a club or group of friends with the same interests. Boys and girls ask each other out and usually split the cost.

CONSOLIDATION AND RECYCLING

BUILDING VOCABULARY

Complete the sentences with words and phrases from the unit.

1. They say _____ . I guess it's true. My sister and her boyfriend are so different!

2. My friend decided to _____ me _____ with a guy from work. What a mistake that was.

3. It's better to turn someone _____ than to go out with someone you don't like.

4. It can be hard to _____ someone out, especially if you're shy.

5. They say _____ are key, so it's important to think about what you do and say the first time you meet someone.

6. If you really liked someone, it can be hard to move _____ after you break up.

7. Some people try speed dating to find a _____ to marry, but others just want to find someone to go out with and have fun.

8. They didn't have anything _____. He was really active, and she was the quiet type.

Work with a partner. Create short exchanges using the words and phrases from the unit and from other units.

Example:
Student A: What do you think about going out
*   on a blind date?*
Student B: It's kind of risky.
Student A: Do you really think so? Why?

WRITING

Write a letter to the editor.
Choose one of the following topics.
Use words and expressions from this unit.

- What displays of affection are appropriate in public?
- Should people of different backgrounds, race, ethnicities, or faiths date?
- Speed dating and online dating — are these the future of dating?

Then exchange letters with a classmate.
Reply to your classmate's letter as if you were the editor.

Quick Fact
Central and South America: Dating is not common until age 15. Most boys and girls date in large groups, going to weekend dance parties or gathering at local clubs.

REFLECTION

1. What is dating?
2. What has had the most impact on our dating practices?
3. How have your views about dating changed from the beginning of the unit?

UNIT 14

Parenting

Philip is starting a website for fathers to share their experiences about parenting. He wants to be as open as possible, but without embarrassing his family. He would like to know what you think of the text for his blog-style home page.

When I finished university, I told everyone that I'd never have kids. At the time, I felt that kids would stop me from being free to follow my dreams, but then I met Sally and my life changed forever. Within three years, we were married and had two kids. Though I love my family, I do wonder sometimes what I'd be doing now if I didn't have children.

There is no doubt that having children is a huge financial burden. Just providing the basic needs – things like clothes, food, shelter, and healthcare can be a struggle sometimes. We always seem to be living on the edge, financially, even with both of us working full time.

As they get older, it doesn't get any easier. My 13-year-old daughter is now coming under more peer pressure to try things I disagree with. She's always saying things like, "But Sarah does it" and "Jane's parents bought one for her." Now, her best friends have the latest mobile phones with videos and MP3 players etc, but that's out of the question for us. We simply can't afford one and if we could, I'd have one!

We've started to try to get them to take more financial responsibility, but they can't earn much juggling school and their part-time jobs; certainly not enough for everything kids need or want nowadays. At least they're learning things like saving, budgeting, and prioritizing.

With children, there's always something to worry about. We worry about whether they are studying enough, getting enough exercise, whether their friends are a good influence. We often talk about how to keep our children out of harm's way, but without smothering them or leaving them more vulnerable to dangerous situations in the long run.

As they get older, it gets even more difficult. We want them to develop and become independent, but we are still responsible if they get into trouble. I try to give them guidance without being over-protective and that's a very fine line.

In a way, I think that my parents were luckier. They didn't have to worry about things like, violent video games, or using the Internet too much.

It seems so much more difficult to teach morals and ethics to children in today's world where they're exposed to so many different influences and values seem to be constantly shifting.

I feel that I'm never more than one step ahead of my kids and often I just have to make things up as I go along. I wish kids came with an instruction manual – I hope that's what this website will develop into.

VOCABULARY

Here are some words that will be useful in this unit. How many do you know? Work with a partner to figure out the meaning of any words that you don't know.

ethics	juggle	over-protective
financial burden	make (things) up	peer pressure
guidance	morals	protect
in harm's way	out of harm's way	to what extent
influence	out of the question	values

What other words and phrases do you know related to the topic?

VOCABULARY ACTIVITIES

A. Circle the letter of the answer that you think best completes each sentence. Then work with a partner. Take turns reading the sentences. Compare your answers.

1. A major strain for parents is _____ .
   a. paying all the costs of raising children.   b. deciding what to name a child.

2. If someone is in harm's way, that person might _____ .
   a. cause problems.   b. get hurt.

3. _____ in particular are very influenced by peer pressure.
   a. Parents   b. Teenagers

4. If parents are legally responsible, they can be _____ if their child breaks the law.
   a. fined or go to prison   b. given support

5. When you live on the edge, you _____ .
   a. just manage to get by.   b. you get by with no problem.

B. Work with a partner. Answer the questions.

1. What are some examples of strains on parents or children?
2. What are some ways a parent can be over-protective?
3. What are two values that are important for parents to teach their children?

GRAPHIC ORGANIZER

Think about your parents and the parents of people you know.
What kind of parent will you be? Fill in the chart. Then work with a partner and compare your ideas.

I WOULD...	I WOULD NOT...

POINTS OF VIEW *Should parents be punished for the actions of their kids?*

PRE-LISTENING QUESTIONS

1. Who do you think is responsible for teaching children right from wrong?
2. Who should be punished if children do something wrong?
3. Have you ever been punished for something you didn't do?

SITUATION: *Emily has just heard some troubling news.*

Tom	Emily, you look upset. What's wrong?
Emily	I just found out that my brother has to go to parenting classes and pay a fine because his son was caught stealing candy. I can't believe it – that my nephew would steal, or that my brother has to pay for it.
Tom	Well, it sort of makes sense. Being the parent, he's responsible for his child's actions. Don't get me wrong, I'm not saying your brother is a bad parent, but it is the parents who are supposed to teach their children what's right and wrong.
Emily	I know my nephew. He's a good kid. I can't imagine him ever stealing something. Even if he did, he's the one who deserves to be punished. He needs to be held responsible for his own actions, not my brother.
Tom	But he's only a kid. Kids make mistakes.
Emily	Yes, but he needs to understand that there are consequences to his actions.
Tom	If I were your brother, I'd just go to the parenting classes and see if I got any good ideas. I know I'm clueless about parenting. Then, I would make my son pay me back for the fine. He would have to take some responsibility for what he did.
Emily	Yeah, that might work. I guess it just bothers me that my brother didn't do anything wrong yet he's being punished for something his son did.
Tom	I can see your point, but then whose responsibility is it to teach children right from wrong? They're not born knowing it.
Emily	No, and parents play a large role in that teaching, but so do teachers, friends, and society in general. How can you hold only parents responsible when there are so many other influences on children these days? It just isn't right.

CHECK FOR UNDERSTANDING

1. What two things have upset Emily?
2. Why does Emily think the decision is wrong?
3. Why does Tom disagree with Emily?
4. Who do you agree with more, Tom or Emily?

Work with a partner. Compare your answers.

Quick Fact
Parental responsibility legislation has been enacted in three Canadian provinces: Manitoba (1997), Ontario (2000), and British-Columbia (2001).

PERSONALIZATION

Complete these sentences with your own ideas.

> *I can't believe...*
> *I can't imagine...*
> *Parents are supposed to teach their children...*
> *I think... ought to be responsible for...*
> *I'm clueless about...*

Now share your sentences with a classmate.

DISCUSSION STRATEGIES - Giving advice

Giving advice can be difficult. The person you're talking to may not want to hear what you have to say. Here are some "gentle" ways to give advice.

> I think you ought to/should...
>
> Maybe you should consider _____ing...
>
> If I were you, I'd...
>
> What if you...?
>
> You could (always)...
>
> I'm told that... is good.
>
> Try…

Discussion Strategy in Action

A. Read the sentences below. Then listen to the advice given. For each speaker, decide what the advice is about and write the correct letter in the blank.

1. _____   a. My son won't listen to me. I need a way to punish him.

2. _____   b. I just got a great job offer, but my parents don't want me to take it.

3. _____   c. I only have one child and I'm worried she'll be lonely.

4. _____   d. My parents don't like my new girlfriend.

5. _____   e. My daughter has no idea how to manage money.

B. Work with a partner and give your own advice for the given situation.

Discussion Practice

Work with a partner. Imagine your friend tells you both that his child wants to go to a very competitive university. What advice would you give, based on the university system in your own country?

> **Brainstorming:**
> What should he/she study?
> Are there any special classes he/she should take?

FURTHER ACTIVITIES

ROLE PLAY

What advice might you give to your child if he or she were in the following situations?

- Your child just got dumped by his or her boy/girlfriend.
- Your child really likes a girl or boy who doesn't seem interested.
- Your child doesn't know what he or she wants to do for a job.
- Your child is too busy and not getting enough sleep.

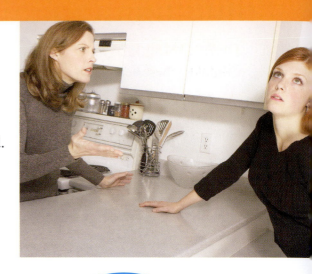

Student A: You are a child. Pick one of the situations above and tell your mother/father about it.

Student B: You are the parent trying to give advice to your son or daughter.

Take turns choosing different situations. Think of other situations.

Quick Fact
The introduction of the one child policy in 1979 has had a big impact on parenting in China.

ACTIVITY

Read and complete the questionnaire.

	AGREE	DISAGREE	NO OPINION
1. If you take care of everything for your children, you're not helping them in the long run.			
2. In general, children are selfish.			
3. At some stage, most children say they dislike their parents.			
4. Parents shouldn't try to be a friend to their children.			
5. Children should be taught not to question their parents' judgment.			
6. In general, mothers nurture children and fathers impose discipline.			
7. It is never acceptable to hit a child.			
8. It is more important to set a good example than to give children lots of rules.			

Work in groups. Compare you answers.

SPEECHES - Story telling

Parents often tell stories to children at night. These stories often have a moral. They teach a lesson, such as "it is better to give than to receive."

Think about the kind of message or moral that you might want to teach a child. Then think of a short story that will illustrate it. Tell the story to a small group or to the class. Can they work out what the message is?

CONSOLIDATION AND RECYCLING

BUILDING VOCABULARY

Fill in the blanks with the correct forms of the words.

NOUN	VERB	ADJECTIVE	ADVERB
protection			-
responsibility	-		
	intend		
prevention			-
	-	ethical	
	strain		
	-	universal	
guidance		-	-

Work with a partner. Choose a word from the chart for your partner to use in a sentence. Take turns.

WRITING

Read this letter to an advice column. Write a reply giving your advice.

My son finished university two months ago. He got a business degree from an excellent university. We worked hard to send him there so that he would have the opportunities that we never had. Before he even graduated, he was offered a good job with an international computer company. Then last week, he announced that he didn't want to go into business and has just got a job as a disk jockey at a small local radio station. We are horrified after all the work that has gone into getting him this far. We worry about his future. He is very sensitive about this and doesn't want to discuss it. What should we do?

Share your reply with your classmates. Discuss each other's ideas.

REFLECTION

1. What challenges do parents face?
2. How do the challenges change as children get older?
3. If you were going to give someone advice about being a parent, what would you say?

UNIT 15

Natural Disasters

EARTHQUAKES

Earthquakes happen frequently. Usually they are harmless, either because they are small, or because they happen far from people and buildings. Sometimes though, these natural hazards are big enough to have the potential to devastate large areas. A strong earthquake occurring near a large city can cause many deaths, injuries, and widespread destruction of property. One of the most serious earthquakes ever was in Shaanxi, China in 1556 where, according to historical records, 830,000 people died.

It is often not the earthquake, but what happens afterwards that may have as big an impact as the earthquake itself and lead to a significant loss of life. The death toll in the Shaanxi quake includes those who died later from disease and hardship resulting directly from the earthquake.

A strong earthquake underwater can cause a tsunami, a series of powerful waves. In December 2004, a very strong earthquake, measuring 9.1 on the Richter scale, occurred near Indonesia. The resulting tsunami killed 230,000 people all along the Indian Ocean coast.

In 1970, an earthquake off the coast of Peru caused an enormous landslide. The rocks and ice that fell from the surrounding mountains quickly buried the town of Yungay and killed over 20,000 people.

Fires are another hazard associated with earthquakes. They can be even more devastating than the quake. When San Francisco, USA was hit by an earthquake in 1906, damaged gas pipes caused fires which could not be put out quickly because water supply pipes had also been severed by the earthquake. The fires burned wildly for three days destroying two-thirds of the city, including the entire business district.

We may know where an earthquake is likely to happen, but we are rarely able to predict when. It is the lack of adequate warning that makes them particularly dangerous. An earthquake in Tangshan, China in 1976 occurred when everyone was still asleep. Later, while people were digging in the rubble to find survivors, there was an aftershock, a minor earthquake following the main earthquake. This killed many of the people who were trapped, as well as some of those trying to rescue them.

We can't prevent earthquakes so the challenge is to find ways to reduce risks so that they don't automatically result in disasters. We can control the outcome to some extent by preparing for an earthquake. We can avoid building in areas where earthquakes are common, or at least ensure that the cities are designed so that the utilities are less likely to be damaged or can be repaired easily and the buildings are constructed in a way that prevents them from suddenly collapsing even in a strong earthquake.

VOCABULARY

Here are some words that will be useful in this unit. How many do you know? Work with a partner to figure out the meaning of any words that you don't know.

collapse	hazard	rubble
death toll	hurricane	significant
destroy	impact	survivors
devastate	landslide	tsunami
earthquake	outcome	typhoon
hardship	potential	volcano

What other words and phrases do you know related to the topic?

VOCABULARY ACTIVITIES

A. Match each word from column A with the word or phrase closest in meaning from column B.

Column A		Column B
1. devastating	___	a. influence, effect
2. hardship	___	b. broken parts of buildings that have been destroyed
3. collapse	___	c. the chance that some thing bad may happen
4. impact	___	d. fall down suddenly
5. rubble	___	e. very destructive
6. potential	___	f. something that makes life difficult

B. Fill in the gaps. Use words from the vocabulary list above. Remember to use the correct word form.

1. When the _____ struck, a huge wave crashed into the buildings along the coast.
2. The _____ of the strong earthquake was huge and led to many hardships.
3. Fire can _____ many buildings very quickly.
4. An earthquake always has the _____ to cause a disaster, but not all earthquakes harm people.
5. After the earthquake, people were digging to rescue the _____ still trapped in the rubble.

Work with a partner. Take turns. Say a word related to natural disasters. Your partner will make a sentence.

GRAPHIC ORGANIZER

Fill in the blanks with any information you already know. Then work with a partner and compare your ideas.

NATURAL EVENTS	WHAT HAPPENS	DESCRIPTIVE WORDS
Earthquakes	*the ground shakes*	
Tsunamis		
Volcanic eruptions		
Typhoons		

PRE-LISTENING QUESTIONS

1. What natural disasters might threaten your home?
2. What would you do if your home were destroyed in a natural disaster?
3. What would you do if you were told you couldn't rebuild?

SITUATION: *Julie can't understand why people take risks.*

Julie	Why do people keep building houses in a place where they're just going to get destroyed? It seems wrong.
Lara	Yes, but most natural disasters are pretty rare though. You can't expect people to stop building on the coast just because there may be a tsunami sometime in the next 100 years.
Julie	Sure, but people are building in places that often have floods, or are near active volcanoes, or on a fault line. Seriously, if I knew there was a risk of flooding or worse, there's no way I would build my house anywhere near that place.
Lara	I know, but it's not always that simple. You have to weigh the risks and take precautions.
Julie	Yes, but even then you can't possibly plan for everything. Remember New Orleans in 2005? It was hurricane season and most people had boarded up their windows and older buildings had been evacuated. But, the hurricane shifted suddenly and caused a huge disaster in a city that wasn't expecting to be hit.
Lara	Yes, but people have lived there for hundreds of years without any problems. Plus, a lot of people had heard the warnings, but ignored them or didn't react properly.
Julie	The authorities should have been better prepared. New Orleans is on the coast and below sea level. It was only a matter of time before something bad happened. It'll happen again one day, too, so it just seems wrong to rebuild there now.
Lara	Well, it was the flooding that followed the hurricane that caused the most damage. That could have been avoided. That was a man-made problem. The city should be rebuilt. It was such a beautiful city. They just need to rebuild smarter.
Julie	All the same, I'd think twice before moving there.
Lara	Well, for a lot of people, there's no real choice. And if someone said, "I'm really sorry, but this place you've called home all your life; you can't stay here anymore." Think about it, what would you do?

CHECK FOR UNDERSTANDING

1. How does Lara feel about rebuilding?
2. How does Julie feel about rebuilding?
3. Do you think Lara can change Julie's mind? Why? Why not?
4. What would you do if someone said, "I'm really sorry, but you can't stay here anymore."

Work with a partner. Compare your answers.

> **Quick Fact**
> Hurricane Katrina caused damage estimated at $100 billion.

PRACTICE AND DISCUSSION

PERSONALIZATION

Complete these sentences with your own ideas.

> *You can't possibly plan for...*
> *No one should...*
> *It just seems wrong to...*
> *If I knew..., I wouldn't*
> *What would you do if....*

Now share your sentences with a classmate.

DISCUSSION STRATEGIES - Giving bad news

FORMAL

I regret to inform you that...

Unfortunately...

I'm (really) sorry, but...

I hate to say it/tell you this, but...

I'm just going to come out and tell you...

So here's the deal...

INFORMAL

Discussion Strategy in Action

Listen. You will hear five situations where someone is giving bad news. Decide if the news is given in an informal or formal way. Write down what happened. Then guess who the speaker is.

	Formality	What happened?	Who is the speaker?
1.	informal / formal		
2.	informal / formal		
3.	informal / formal		
4.	informal / formal		
5.	informal / formal		

Work with a partner. Take turns telling each other some bad news.

Discussion Practice

Work with a partner. Imagine there is a large fire and people are not allowed to go to their houses. The roads are closed. It is a very dangerous situation. People must wait at a nearby school. What would a police officer say to someone who has two dogs at their house and wants to try to rescue them? Think of other similar situations and what people would say.

FURTHER ACTIVITIES

ROLE PLAY

Student A: A strong typhoon is coming. You only have a couple of days to get ready. You must convince your partner to prepare for it. You plan to stay, but suggest that your partner should leave.

   Examples: Buy enough food and bottled water to last you for a week.

Student B: You aren't worried about the typhoon. Tell Student A why the advice won't work or is unnecessary.

   Examples: I hate to tell you this, but I can't. I don't have enough money.

> **Brainstorming:**
>
> Think of dangerous situations people need to prepare for.
>
> Think of what you would say to convince people to prepare.
>
> Think of what you would do if someone told you to leave.

ACTIVITY

Emergency planning can help prevent natural disasters.
Brainstorm ways that countries, cities, and families can be better prepared. Be specific.

- What should a country do? What should a city do?
- What should emergency personnel such as police and firefighters do?
- What should individual families do?
- If you were going to make a survival kit for you and your family what would you include?

Share your ideas with your classmates.

SPEECHES - Weather report

You are a weather forecaster. A heat wave is expected to get worse in your area. It has been much hotter than normal for a long time and could soon start to get very dangerous. Forest fires have already started to get out of control.
Consider:

- what the potential dangers are
- what people should do to prepare for them

Discuss your ideas with a partner. Then create your own 1 – 2 minute broadcast.

Quick Fact
According to a UN agency, the International Strategy for Disaster Reduction, global warming could be putting more people at risk from natural disasters.

CONSOLIDATION AND RECYCLING

BUILDING VOCABULARY

1. Use the vocabulary from the unit to complete the announcement below.

I regret to inform you that we have received reports of an _____ earlier this morning in northern India that measured 7.7 on the _____ scale. There were several _____ as well and people are obviously very frightened as buildings continue to shake. Many buildings have _____ and several roads were destroyed. People are now digging through the _____ searching for _____ . The _____ of the earthquake will be felt for a while. The earthquake occurred at 10:32 am. Fortunately, most people were away from their homes, at work in the fields, so the authorities do not expect the _____ toll to be very high. However, the government is expecting diseases and _____ for people until they can get food, water, and other emergency supplies brought in. It will be a while before they can rebuild and their lives return to normal.

2. Now work in a group. Imagine you work for an international aid organization. You have ten million dollars to use to help the people in India.

Decide how the money should be used. It could be used for immediate relief, for example, providing shelter, food, and water and medical care, or for longer term projects, for example, building roads, schools, and other buildings.

WRITING

Imagine you are in the middle of a heavy snowstorm, a typhoon, a drought, or another natural disaster. Describe the experience.

- What do you see?
- What is happening?
- How do you feel?
- Are other people around? How are they reacting?
- Are they doing anything to help one another?

Write a description. Share it with your classmates.

Quick Fact
Many fatalities from earthquakes occur when people run outside of buildings only to be killed by falling debris from collapsing walls.

REFLECTION

1. Is there anywhere on Earth that is safe from a natural disaster?
2. How much do you think we should worry about natural disasters?
3. Do you know if there is an emergency plan where you live? How can you find out?

Multiple Intelligences

Read the quiz and label each box with the correct intelligence.

Word smart	**Number smart**	**Body smart**	**People smart**
Music smart	**Picture smart**	**Self smart**	**Nature smart**

Then answer the quiz questions to find out what your dominant intelligences are. Read each statement. Write the number that best represents your response next to each statement. Total the number for each category. The categories with the higher totals represent your stronger intelligences. Compare your results with a partner or in a small group.

1 Not at all like me   4 A lot like me
2 A little like me   5 Definitely me
3 Somewhat like me

A _____ **smart**
Total Score

I enjoy doing crossword puzzles and other word games. ☐
I write in a journal regularly. ☐
I like to read. ☐
I enjoy having discussions. ☐

B _____ **smart**
Total Score

I often find myself tapping my fingers or moving my legs. ☐
I like to work with my hands. ☐
I understanding best by doing. ☐
I prefer to be actively involved rather than watching. ☐

C _____ **smart**
Total Score

I like to sing. ☐
To help me remember things, I make up a rhyme. ☐
I can easily follow the beat of the music. ☐
I can play a musical instrument. ☐

D _____ **smart**
Total Score

I know how I will react to most situations. ☐
I prefer to spend time alone. ☐
I work best on my own. ☐
I have a good understanding of my feelings. ☐

E _____ **smart**
Total Score

I like math/science. ☐
I keep a "things to do list". ☐
I work best in an organized area. ☐
I need to have a diary or schedule. ☐

F _____ **smart**
Total Score

I like to work in groups. ☐
I enjoy sharing my thoughts and feelings with others. ☐
I like learning about different cultures. ☐
I prefer to participate in team sports rather than individual ones. ☐

G _____ **smart**
Total Score

I remember things best by seeing them. ☐
I can read maps and charts easily. ☐
I have a good sense of direction. ☐
I like to draw and paint. ☐

H _____ **smart**
Total Score

I prefer to spend my time outdoors rather than indoors. ☐
I notice trees, plants, flowers and other things in nature. ☐
I have a collection (shells, rocks, stamps, cards, etc.). ☐
I learn best when I can go on field trips to explore and observe nature exhibits, museums, or the outdoors. ☐

My highest score ☐   My lowest score ☐

Dating

Are you best suited for conventional dating, online dating, or speed dating? Take the quiz to find out.

1 The best way to find a potential partner is:
   a. through friends/parents.
   b. through the Internet.
   c. through a dating service.

2 Which way do you feel most comfortable expressing yourself?
   a. In writing.
   b. Face to face.
   c. Over the phone.

3 When you meet someone, you are first attracted to:
   a. appearance.
   b. personality.
   c. both.

4 "Love at first sight."
   a. Does not exist.
   b. Happens everyday.
   c. Is possible.

5 Who should pay for a date?
   a. The person who asked.
   b. Each person should pay half.
   c. The man.

6 When you go on a date, are you looking to:
   a. casually date?
   b. date someone seriously?
   c. get married soon?

7 Your ideal date includes:
   a. going out with a group of people.
   b. meeting in a virtual café.
   c. going to dinner followed by a walk on the beach.

8 For a lasting relationship it's better if:
   a. you have little in common — it keeps the relationship exciting.
   b. you know nothing about each other beforehand.
   c. you have a lot in common — the more things you share the better.

9 Describe your availability to go on dates.
   a. I have a lot of time to date.
   b. I don't have any time to date.
   c. It's easier if it's part of my other activities.

10 Having your parents' approval of the person you date is:
   a. very important.
   b. important, but not all I consider.
   c. not something I care about too much.

	a	b	c		a	b	c
1.	1	3	5	6.	3	5	1
2.	3	5	1	7.	5	3	1
3.	5	3	1	8.	1	3	5
4.	3	5	1	9.	1	5	3
5.	3	5	1	10.	1	5	3

Look at your answers and add up your score. Then find the description that matches your score.

0 - 16 points You are a conventional dater. You prefer to meet people through traditional, trusted sources, such as parents and friends, and it's important that your parents like your partner. You enjoy creating romantic dates such as candlelit dinners and walks on a beach. You have a lot of free time to meet people. You are looking for a serious relationship, possibly marriage.

17 - 33 points You are an Internet dater. You communicate best in writing. You focus more on building an emotional and intellectual connection over appearance. You have a busy schedule and can make time to date if it's part of your activities. You like the adventure and anonymity of the online world. You don't care what your parents think. You just want to date casually, nothing serious.

34 - 50 points You are a speed dater. Love at first sight exists for you. You don't have very much free time so having as many dates as possible will give you greatest chance of having that 'special moment'. You need all the help you can get. You prefer to communicate with people face to face and you often judge them on appearance.

Does this quiz accurately describe you? Why or why not?

PATTERNS & COLLOCATIONS

FEATURED MOVIES

Unit 1 Dress Code (p 06)
The Devil Wears Prada (2006)
Anne Hathaway, Stanley Tucci
Director: David Frankel
Credit: 20th Century Fox / The Kobal Collection and Barry Wetcher

Andrea is hired to work for the head of a fashion magazine. She knows nothing of the fashion industry and has no fashion sense. She is forced to change her simple and plain style, for a more trendy and elegant one, in order to gain the acceptance of her ruthless boss and colleagues. However, with her new appearance, she changes her attitude and behavior and starts to lose her friends; she seems more preoccupied about her image and her future in the magazine.

- -

Unit 2 Video Games (p 12)
Final Fantasy: The Spirits Within (2001)
Credit:Chris Lee Prod/Square Co / The Kobal Collection

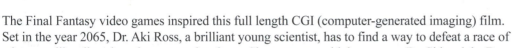

The Final Fantasy video games inspired this full length CGI (computer-generated imaging) film. Set in the year 2065, Dr. Aki Ross, a brilliant young scientist, has to find a way to defeat a race of phantom-like aliens in order to save the planet. She teams up with her mentor Dr. Sid and the Deep Eyes military squadron, led by Grey Edwards. But as they all work toward a peaceful end, another military leader, General Hein, devises a plot to eradicate the aliens that risks destructing the planet.

- -

Unit 3 Advertising (p 18)
Thank You for Smoking (2005)
William H Macy
Director: Jason Reitman
Credit: Fox Searchlight / The Kobal Collection

Nick Naylor is a lobbyist for the tobacco industry. His job is to promote cigarette smoking - a seemingly impossible task in a time when the health hazards are well known. Nick is good at his job though. He argues well and manages to portray his clients as the victims. However, he has to work hard to get his son to understand and respect his work. When a news reporter betrays Nick's trust, his world seems in danger of collapsing.

- -

Unit 4 International Competitions (p 24)
Endurance (1999)
Haile Gebreselassie
Director: Bud Greenspan & Leslie Woodhead
Credit: The Kobal Collection

Haile Gebreselassie was one of the greatest long distance runners of all time. Despite the hardships he faced growing up in a large, poor family in rural Ethiopia, he won the gold medal for the men's 10,000-meter race at the 1996 Atlanta Olympics, taking him instantly from anonymous third world poverty to international celebrity. His father wanted him to stay and work on the farm, but in 1980, Miruts Yifter won the 10,000-meter race at the Moscow Olympics and Haile became determined to do the same.

- -

Unit 5 Mobile Phones (p 30)
Cellular (2004)
Chris Evans
Director: David R Ellis
Credit: New Line/Electric Entertainment / The Kobal Collection / Richard Foremant

Jessica, has been kidnapped by men who want something from her husband. There's a phone in the room where she is held captive, but it has been smashed by one of the kidnappers. Jessica fits some of the parts back together and crosses wires to make a call - at random. She gets through to Ryan, a young man who at first doesn't believe her. He agrees not to hang up and takes the phone to the police. Hearing Jessica's conversation with her captor he realizes her family is in danger so he tries to help them. However, she doesn't know where she is and his phone's battery might die soon.

Unit 6 Manners and Ettiquette (p 36)
The Princess Diaries (2001)
Larry Miller, Anne Hathaway, Julie Andrews
Director: Garry Marshall
Credit: Brownhouse Prod./BOTNP Inc / The Kobal Collection . Ron Batzdorff

Mia is an awkward, but very bright 15-year-old girl being raised by a single mom in San Francisco, USA. What she doesn't know is that she is also the daughter of the Prince of Genovia. Genovia is a small European country and when the prince dies unexpectedly, Mia must make a choice between continuing the carefree life of an American teen or taking on the responsibilities of the throne. While Mia contemplates her future, she takes lessons in manners and etiquette from her grandmother, the queen.

Unit 7 Volunteering (p 42)
Pay it Forward (2000)
Haley Joel Osment
Director: Mimi Leder
Credit: Bel Air/WB / The Kobal Collection / David James

Trevor has an idea that could change the world: he will do good deeds for three people and instead of paying him back, they each 'pay it forward' by performing good deeds for three new people. In this way, someone does you a good turn, you pass it on to three other people, they pass it on and positive changes occur. Trevors set out to help himself, his mother and his teacher, but his efforts bring a revolution, helping an ever-widening circle of people completely unknown to him.

Unit 8 Health and Nature (p 48)
Who Killed the Electric Car? (2006)
Director: Chris Paine
Credit: Electric Entertainment/Sony / The Kobal Collection

The 'resurrection' of the electric car and hybrid models combining electric and gasoline engines was a reaction to increasing gasoline prices and fossil fuel shortages made worse by unrest in oil producing regions around the world. But could more have been done sooner? The film looks at the actions of the US government, car companies, Big Oil, as well as consumers. By focusing on the electric car the film also considers the role of renewable energy and sustainable living in our future.

Unit 9 Extreme Sports (p 54)
Murderball (2005)
Mark Zurpan and others
Director: Henry Alex Rubin / Dana Adam Shapiro
Credit: MTV Films / The Kobal Collection

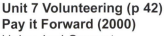

Wheelchair rugby is a full-contact sport - one strategy is to knock over your opponent's chair. "I'm a guy in a chair," one of the players says, "I'm just like you, except I'm sitting down." This documentary follows Team USA during a couple of seasons. The off-court drama is also fraught with tension. Joe was on the American team for many years, but when he is dropped, he gets revenge by becoming the coach of the Canadian team. Canada then beats the U.S. for the first time in 12 years.

Unit 10 Free Education (p 60)
Good Will Hunting (1997)
Matt Damon
Director: Gus Van Sant
Credit: Miramax / The Kobal Collection

Professor Lambeau offers a prize to any student who can solve a difficult problem. The next morning, the answer is written on a blackboard, but none of the students claim credit. Lambeau later catches Will Hunting, a college janitor, writing on the board and realizes the poor, working-class young man is a natural math genius who can intuitively see through difficult problems the professor is baffled by. Lambeau wants to help Will, to get the education he deserves.

Unit 11 Multiple Intelligences (p 66)
School of Rock (2003)
Robert Tasi, Joey Gaydos Jr, Jack Black, Kevin Clark, Rebecca Brown
Director: Richard Linklater
Credit: Paramount / The Kobal Collection / Andrew Schwartz

Dewey gets fired from his rock band. As he needs to quickly raise money to pay his rent and other bills, he pretends to be his friend Ned in order to take a job as a 4th grade substitute teacher at an expensive private school. His unorthodox attitude has a powerful effect on his students. Dewey's "school of rock" gives them greater self-esteem and an appreciation of skills beyond the traditionally accepted academic notions of success and failure.

Unit 12 Gender Roles (p 72)
Bend It Like Beckham (2002)
Paraminder K Nagra
Director: Gurinder Chadha
Credit: Bend It Films/Film Council / The Kobal Collection / Christine Parry

The film tells the story of Jessminder, an 18-year-old women who has her heart set on a future in professional soccer. She is very talented, but her parents are uncomfortable with their daughter playing soccer instead of adopting traditional Indian pursuits the family feel are more suitable for a young woman. Jessminder must now decide what's important for her, playing professional soccer, or hanging up her boots, finding a nice boyfriend and learning to cook East Indian recipes perfectly.

Unit 13 Dating (p 78)
Must Love Dogs (2005)
Diane Lane
Director: Garry David Goldberg
Credit: Warner Bros. / The Kobal Collection / Claudette Barius

Sarah Nolan, a preschool teacher in her thirties, is divorced. Her friends and family try to find her a boyfriend, but without success. Her sister turns to the Internet for help. She posts a phony (because everyone lies) singles ad on the Internet on Sarah's behalf. This leads to a series of bad dates, including one with her father who had turned to Internet dating after his wife died. Eventually Sarah finds Jake, her perfect match.

Unit 14 Parenting (p 84)
Freaky Friday (2003)
Lindsay Lohan, Jamie Lee Curtis
Director: Mark Waters
Credit: Walt Disney Pictures / The Kobal Collection / Ron Batzdorf

There is a wide generation gap between Tess Coleman and her fifteen-year-old daughter, Anna. They don't see eye-to-eye on clothes, hair, music, and certainly not in each other's taste in men.
One Thursday night, they have a big argument. Everything changes the next day as they wake to find they have switched bodies. As they adjust to their new personalities, they begin to understand each other more. However, with Tess's wedding scheduled for Saturday, they quickly have to find a way to switch back.

Unit 15 Natural Disasters (p 90)
Dante's Peak (1997)
Director: Roger Donaldson
Credit: Universal / The Kobal Collection / Ben Glass

Harry is sent to the small town of Dante's Peak to check on unusual activity at a nearby volcano. He tries to convince the city council that the volcano is dangerous. However, they are reluctant to declare an emergency as people's safety is set against economical interests. When Dante's peak does erupt, the city panics. Meanwhile, Harry goes to the volcano with Rachel, the town's mayor, to rescue her family. They try to reach safety while the town below is destroyed.

ABOUT THE AUTHORS

Jun Liu

Jun Liu is head of the English department at the University of Arizona as well as Executive Director of the English Language Center, Shantou University, China. His research interests include curriculum development and syllabus design, teacher education, classroom-based second language learning and teaching, and second language reading and writing. He has published in TESOL Quarterly, ELT Journal, Journal of English for Academic Purposes, Journal of Asian Pacific Communication, Asian Journal of English Language Teaching, Language and Intercultural Communication, and Educational Research Quarterly, among others. He is the author of Asian Students' Classroom Communication Patterns in US Universities (Greenwood Publishing Group), and the co-author of Peer Response in Second Language Writing Classrooms (University of Michigan Press). He is co-editor of the Michigan Series on Teaching Multilingual Writers. He is also a columnist for "English Teachers" in the 21st Century Weekly in China and editor of Review of Applied Linguisties in China (Higher Education Press).

A recipient of the TESOL Newbury House Award for Excellence in Teaching, and co-founder and Past Chair of Non-Native English Speakers in TESOL Caucus (NNEST), he served on the TESOL Board of Directors serving as Director at Large (2001-2004), and was appointed as TESOL representative in China in 2004. Jun Liu was TESOL President (2006-2007).

Tracy S Davis

Tracy earned her Masters in Theoretical Linguistics from Syracuse University, where she specialized in Syntax. She also studied ESOL there, focusing on non-traditional materials in the classroom. Tracy has taught ESOL classes at various levels and spent a year in China, teaching at the English Language Center at Shantou University before returning to the US to undertake a Ph.D. in Applied Linguistics at The Pennsylvania State University. Her research interests include; ESOL teacher training and education; Corpus linguistics; Technology in the Foreign Language Classroom; and ESOL materials creation.

Susanne M Rizzo

Since earning her Masters degree in TESL from Kent State University in Kent, Ohio, Susanne has taught integrated and special skills courses in ESL and EFL settings. She is particularly interested in learner motivation, task-based instruction, and Computer Assisted Language Learning (CALL). In addition, she has co-designed a multi-media online course in American culture and has presented papers at a number of national and international conferences. Susanne has taught at Shantou University's English Language Center in Guangdong Province, P.R. China, and at Koç University English Language Center in Istanbul, Turkey. Susanne has traveled extensively in East Asia and the Middle East.